5 MINUTE PARENTING FIXES

An Hachette UK Company
www.hachette.co.uk

Vie Books, an imprint of Summersdale Publishers Ltd
Part of Octopus Publishing Group Limited
Carmelite House
50 Victoria Embankment
LONDON
EC4Y 0DZ
PO19 1RP
UK

www.summersdale.com

Printed and bound in Poland

ISBN: 978-1-78685-247-2

Substantial discounts on bulk quantities of Summersdale books are available to corporations, professional associations and other organisations. For details contact general enquiries: telephone: +44 (0) 1243 771107 or email: enquiries@summersdale.com.

Disclaimer
The material in this book is not intended as a substitute for the professional advice of a qualified therapist or health-care professional. All children are unique, and while the book offers suggestions and recommendations to parents and other caregivers, we encourage you to use your common sense and judgement to determine when it's appropriate to seek professional guidance.

7–16 years

5 MINUTE PARENTING FIXES

Quick Tips and Advice for the Everyday Challenges of Raising Children

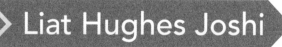

Liat Hughes Joshi

vie

CONTENTS

ABOUT THE AUTHOR

Liat Hughes Joshi is a London-based parenting writer. This is her fifth book.

She has contributed to all the main national newspapers including *The Telegraph*, *The Sunday Times* and *The Sun*, as well as a range of magazines and websites.

She has made TV and radio appearances as a commentator on parenting and family life, including on Sky News, *ITV Tonight*, *Good Morning Britain* and BBC Radio 4 and 5Live.

INTRODUCTION

It's everywhere and it starts from the moment our children are born – sometimes even before they're born. The bombardment of advice on how to parent. It comes from well-meaning relatives, friends or random strangers telling you how you should be dealing with your children. Not to mention the countless pages of blogs, articles and videos if you search online, on every issue about babies through to toddlers and teens.

Therein lies the problem – we're overloaded with child-rearing advice these days. We don't have time to pore over it all. Of course by writing another parenting book, I'm merely adding to this but there's a rationale here: to create a single source of reliable answers to the most common problems we face as parents. Sensible solutions that you can read and digest in a matter of minutes – under five, in fact. You've got better things to do after all – such as raising children.

CHAPTER 1

ENCOURAGING
GOOD BEHAVIOUR

- ► What it means to be an authoritative parent
- ► Why every parent should have a behaviour management plan
- ► Setting family rules
- ► How to deal with a strop
- ► How to get your kids to help around the house
- ► How to instil good manners

WHAT IT MEANS TO BE AN AUTHORITATIVE PARENT

Research shows that the best-behaved, most well-adjusted and independent children tend to come from families with an 'authoritative' parenting style. This is warmer than very strict 'authoritarian' parents and firmer than 'permissive' parents.

Authoritative parents mix warmth with control. They're in charge but in a kind, considerate way which involves their child where appropriate. They seek to explain and educate children about the consequences of their behaviour rather than expecting automatic compliance and obedience.

Authoritative parents say:

'I'll listen to your opinion but I'm a grown-up with more life experience, so the final decision is mine.'

'I understand why you want to do that but I don't think you are ready for it and these are the reasons why... when you're older you can...'

'I know you're tired and frustrated but that sort of behaviour is never acceptable.'

They don't say:

'Do as you're told!' (It's preferable to explain why, not just expect compliance.)

'Respect your elders.' (Surely respect is earned, not automatic – even for parents.)

'You'll get a smack if you do that again.' (Authoritative parents don't smack.)

'It's because he's a boy/she's tired/it's Wednesday.' (They don't make excuses for bad behaviour.)

'If you don't behave I'm cancelling Christmas/that day out.' (Only threaten something you're willing to follow through on.)

WHY EVERY PARENT SHOULD HAVE A BEHAVIOUR MANAGEMENT PLAN

Actively thinking through how you – and ideally their other parent – want to manage your child's behaviour to maximise the good and minimise the bad means you'll feel calmer, more confident and more in control. Plus consistency should lead to improvement because they will know that if they do X, Y will happen. Every time.

What is a behaviour management plan?

OK, OK, this does sound like the sort of jargon a management consultant who's restructuring a company uses, but this term does what it says on the tin. It's a plan of how you're going to manage behaviour. It needn't even be written down or be formal but might involve:

- ▶ Family rules – what you will and won't allow.

- ▶ What happens when the rules are broken or other negative behaviour occurs.

- ▶ What are your rewards and sanctions?
  Will you give warnings?

Why have a plan?

By having a plan in mind, you'll limit the scope for knee-jerk reactions when your child misbehaves or pushes your buttons. This matters because in the heat of the moment, when all that stress-induced cortisol is dashing round your body, we don't always parent as well as we could. We might make false threats we can't deliver on (the classic being 'I'm cancelling Christmas') which mean our children won't take us seriously in the future, or we might be overly harsh or lenient.

If under your plan, you know that if your child does X, you will do Y, you'll feel less stressed, more in control and they'll pick up on this. Of course kids do unpredictable things, but even then, by having a plan, you'll have sensible and familiar actions to draw upon.

SETTING FAMILY RULES

Setting rules can be helpful as children thrive on predictability. The more they know what your expectations are, the better they're likely to behave. Every family and every child will have different rules and norms – it's too individual to prescribe them all but some ideas for areas that rules work in are:

▶ Mealtimes, e.g. 'we come straight to the table when Mum or Dad says that dinner is ready'. 'We don't get up mid-meal.'

▶ Screen use e.g. 'no screens after lights out in your bedroom'.

▶ Politeness and manners, e.g. 'we speak to each other respectfully'.

▶ Sit down together and agree your rules with your child – that's about informing and involving them appropriately, not getting their permission or approval. Write the rules down and stick them on the fridge!

Decide upon your rewards and punishments

▶ Research shows that rewards work better than punishments to manage behaviour. *But* that doesn't mean not punishing bad behaviour! If you don't address something significant, such as hitting a sibling, then your child might feel they can 'get away with it'.

▶ Pick rewards and sanctions that really motivate your child. For a lot of modern kids, it's screen time or pocket money. Alternatives include choosing a film you all watch on a Friday night, a game with you or picking the weekend's takeaway dinner.

▶ If you threaten something, follow through with it or your child won't take you seriously next time. Don't use threats you won't be able to follow through on!

Reward charts work well for younger children – up to around age eight or nine. These should have clear, measurable categories (e.g. 'play with your brother nicely for an hour') for which they get a star, points or a marble in a jar and when they get enough of these, they receive a specific reward. With younger children communicate your reward or sanction fairly quickly after the behaviour concerned; otherwise they might struggle to link the two.

For primary school-age children, look at what their school does with rewards and punishments for inspiration. Do they use football-style red and yellow cards, or have a golden time scheme in place perhaps? Find out how it works and consider creating something similar for home. The consistency will be good for your child.

HOW TO DEAL WITH A STROP

Tantrums are by no means the sole territory of toddlers. Older children (and some adults) can get themselves into a proper tizz when things don't go their way. More often than not, this is a child's 'emotional brain' taking over their rational one – they just can't handle their feelings about what's happening. Here's what you can do when your little one – or not so little teenager – turns into a screaming banshee.

Keep calm

This is undoubtedly stressful for a parent and especially when other people are around – your child having a tantrum can feel embarrassing. Try not to focus on what others think but instead on what will resolve the situation effectively. Take deep breaths or walk away for a little while, if it's safe to do so, so you can collect your thoughts ready to deal with this.

Don't shout back – it isn't going to achieve anything

It will probably just make your child angrier, escalate things and reinforce the idea that it's OK to shout when we're upset.

Stick with a firm, authoritative tone of voice and respond minimally

Calmly acknowledge their issue (assuming you can make out what it is above the cacophony of shouting!) by repeating it to them so they feel heard, 'I know you want more time on the tablet but that isn't possible now.'

Then say something such as, 'I'm not able to listen when you're shouting, come back when you can discuss this calmly.' Don't pander to the tantrum with masses of attention.

Send your child somewhere else to calm down

If you're at home, tell them to go to their room or the hallway until they can sort themselves out. If they're in too much of a state to go, walk away yourself.

Absolutely do not give in to what they want or even make compromises

If you do, they'll learn that to get their way all they need do is throw a strop – that will simply open the door to a lot more of them.

Use humour

This is a tricky balancing act as you could just make your child even more angry but sometimes, especially with teens, finding humour in the situation can ease the tension.

"We're parents, not servants."

Many of us struggle to find the time or patience to teach children to do chores at least fairly properly (i.e. not always as well as an adult might do them). It's easier sometimes to just cave in and do it for them. But some short-term effort on simple everyday tasks, such as showing them how to fold clothes, wash up or cook, brings long-term gains because you'll have more help and your kids will know how to do this stuff for themselves when they leave home. One of our roles as parents should surely be to prepare them for their grown-up life, with the skills to be independent and competent and waiting upon them and picking up their dirty socks isn't doing so.

HOW TO GET YOUR KIDS TO HELP AROUND THE HOUSE

Compared to our own childhoods, where mucking in to clear up was just part of being in the family, modern kids often see housework as parents' jobs. There are clear benefits to them helping out – it's good for them to understand that life involves the dull stuff too, it prepares them to be more capable when they leave home, and perhaps best of all for us parents, many hands make light work – the more they do the less we need to do.

Don't nag – have a fresh start

Kids not used to lifting a finger beyond swiping upon screens or tapping TV remote control buttons? It's tempting to nag but instead, sit them down calmly and explain why they need to help more and allocate jobs. Agree rewards if you feel the need (some parents link chores to pocket money or screen use). Turning the modem off until chores are done galvanises most offspring into action and is worth considering. It won't make you popular but you're parenting not participating in a popularity contest.

'Gamify' jobs

Let's face it, chores aren't fun whatever one's age, but you can make them more appealing by turning them into games. How quickly can they empty the dishwasher – can they beat their previous best time or finish before the timer buzzes (without accidentally stabbing the cat with a dropped fork or breaking the china)? Get younger kids playing 'match the socks' with the laundry. Who can tidy their room quickest but to standard?

Give chore choices

Let your kids have some say in what they do – 'would you prefer to gather the dirty washing up or vacuum?', so that they feel involved. If they give the smart-ass answer of 'neither', that's fine – you'll choose for them. Savvy parents might stick an off-putting job in the options to get them to plump for the lesser of two evils: 'would you rather clean the toilet bowl with an old toothbrush... or fetch the laundry?' Tough call...

Have a daily 'team tidy up'

A short blitz every day – say ten minutes – employs the 'many hands make light work' approach and means it doesn't eat into activities they'd rather be doing too much. Stick some music on and let each family member take turns to choose the day's tidying tunes.

Make chores part of their regular routine

Chores done regularly at specific times or on particular days should, in theory, require less nagging – tidying their bedroom on Saturday afternoons, or gathering up dirty clothes after their bath or shower, just becomes routine. Reinforce this by creating a chore chart or timetable as a visual reminder.

Give specific instructions

'Tidy your room' is too vague for children – more defined instructions work better, such as: 'put your books on the shelves, the dirty clothes in the basket and the toys back in the box.' Word requests carefully too; don't say 'please can you do X for me'. The 'for me' implies it's really your job. It's not. You're a family and should all help out.

Chores by age group

Of course, you'll know your own child's capabilities best but as a guide…

Five to seven-year-olds should be able to:

- ▶ Help with dusting
- ▶ Gather up dirty laundry and assist with sorting it out, e.g. matching socks
- ▶ Set the table for dinner

Older primary-school-age children:

- ▶ Make a sandwich or snack
- ▶ Vacuum or sweep the floor
- ▶ Set the table and clear dishes post-meal
- ▶ Wash up
- ▶ Empty the dishwasher

Teenagers:

- ▶ Mow the lawn and weed flowerbeds
- ▶ Wash the car
- ▶ Cook a basic meal
- ▶ Do the laundry

Household tasks to equip your child with by the time they leave home

- ► Laundry: work out the basics of the washing machine, decipher garment washing labels and iron a shirt.

- ► Cooking: plan and make at least a handful of simple meals and grasp the basics of food hygiene.

- ► Cleaning: how to clean a bathroom, kitchen and living room and how to change bedding.

- ► Simple household maintenance: how to change a lightbulb and wire a plug.

HOW TO INSTIL GOOD MANNERS

Society as a whole has seen a relaxation of manners and etiquette for children as well as adults. Youngsters are no longer expected to vacate a seat on the bus for an able-bodied adult, tend to be on first-name-only terms with grown-ups (other than teachers), and few of us worry about elbows resting on dining tables and the like.

Yet some manners remain relevant – they're about respect and consideration for others and we're judged on them in social, romantic and professional situations.

As parents we have to work out which ones matter so that our children can tread on the right side of the line between relaxed informality and rudeness.

What you can do

Drop the nagging and explain why manners are important

Nagging and blindly expecting your kids to stick with etiquette for the sake of it won't work as well as explaining why a particular behaviour matters.

'It's not nice to watch the contents of your mouth when you're chewing,' instead of, 'Don't eat with your mouth open!' Use 'If you look at me when I'm talking to you, I know you're listening,' not 'Look at me when I'm talking to you.'

Say 'If you run around in this cafe, you might crash into a waiter carrying hot drinks,' instead of 'Stop running around.'

Be realistic rather than expecting perfect etiquette all the time

Trying to enforce 1950s finishing school standards of etiquette is likely to be tiresome for you and your children, as well as unnecessary these days. Start with the essentials (see page 31).

Allow older children to discern when they need to be on 'best behaviour'

Children aged over six or seven can usually understand when they need their best manners and when they can relax things. So they will start to remember that whilst it's OK to eat pizza with their fingers at home, at that smart Italian restaurant with the grandparents, it's knife and fork time.

Be a positive role model

If you tend to talk with a mouth full of food, you can't expect your child not to. If you're disrespectful to shop or restaurant staff, what will they pick up? Children learn by copying.

There's a difference between respecting everyone and behaving respectfully

The idea that children should automatically respect their elders is rather outdated. That said, even if someone is behaving badly or has views your child disagrees with, they can still *behave* respectfully and politely towards them.

Build general awareness of other people's needs

Younger children aren't always the best at being aware of their impact on others, especially when they're excited or engrossed in something. Help them learn to respond to their environment for themselves, e.g. keeping their volume down in a quiet doctor's waiting room or not hurtling around a busy restaurant.

Modern manners: which ones still matter?

General

- ▶ Saying please and thank you.

- ▶ Looking people in the eye when conversing.

- ▶ Paying attention to guests at home, dinner companions when dining out and when at someone else's house, rather than looking at a gadget.

- ▶ Showing gratitude for a gift or food someone has made.

- ▶ Not talking over people or interrupting too much.

- ▶ Behaving vaguely sensibly in public areas that aren't designed for playing – no running around getting in people's way or being unduly noisy.

- ▶ Apologising if they hurt someone or damage something.

Bodily manners

- ▶ Discussing toilet issues only where directly relevant or appropriate.

- ▶ Not passing wind or belching loudly in public.

- ▶ Wiping snotty noses with tissues – not sleeves or hands.

- ▶ Covering mouths when sneezing or yawning.

Table manners

- ▶ Not eating with mouth gaping open to display the contents or talking with their mouth full.

- ▶ Staying at the table during meals.

- ▶ Not taking food from others' plates unless they've given permission or leaning across someone's meal.

- ▶ Using a knife and fork unless it's a food that's normally eaten with fingers (e.g. burgers, sandwiches).

- ▶ Eating in a measured way – no licking plates or bowls!

Take a step back now and then – a bit like an appraisal at work – and assess where you're at with your child's behaviour and family life generally. Whether you do this just as parents or with your child there, or indeed both, is personal choice. Ask questions such as:

- What's going well and not so well?

- What are the flashpoints that are triggering any arguments, tension or tantrums?

- Are they starting to spend too much time on screens?

- How are their friendships and other relationships going?

- Are they doing as well at school as their potential suggests?

- Do you need to change the behaviour management plan – adjust the rewards or sanctions? Or change any of the family rules?

Taking time to evaluate your children's behaviour will help everyone avoid slipping into bad habits and allow you to nip problems in the bud.

Often with parenting there's an element of 'long-term pain for short-term gain'. To really sort something out you have to invest time especially when it comes to breaking habits or changing behaviour. Initially it might be harder work than not addressing the issue but it will be worth it in the end.

CHAPTER 2

MENTAL HEALTH
AND WELL-BEING

- ▶ My child is anxious
- ▶ My child seems depressed
- ▶ Essential things needed to help your child become a happy, well-functioning adult
- ▶ Building positive self-image
- ▶ Dealing with gender issues
- ▶ My child is lying
- ▶ My child has a fear or phobia
- ▶ Stress busters for kids

MY CHILD IS ANXIOUS

ABOUT ANXIETY IN CHILDREN:

Anxiety can be defined as feelings of unease, worry and/or fear.

Common triggers are:

- ▶ exams

- ▶ moving house or school

- ▶ family separation and divorce

- ▶ serious illness or bereavement

- ▶ bullying and friendship problems

- ▶ body changes during adolescence.

Signs your child is anxious:

It's natural to worry sometimes but if your child's concerns are overwhelming or interfering with everyday life, there could be something more serious going on. Anxiety can cause both physical and emotional symptoms, such as:

- ▶ irritability, tearfulness or anger

- ▶ episodes of feeling panicked and/or breathless

- ▶ difficulty sleeping or eating

- ▶ stomach upsets or aches

- ▶ bed-wetting

- ▶ problems concentrating

- ▶ loss of enthusiasm for their usual interests

- ▶ overwhelmingly negative thinking

- ▶ being unusually withdrawn.

[source: www.mind.org.uk]

TIP: Help your child understand these signs so they recognise what is happening to them when they feel anxious and can ask for help.

[source: NHS.uk]

FACT: One in ten children have a diagnosable mental health disorder and one in four of all children show some evidence of mental ill health.

[source: www.youngminds.org.uk]

What you can do:

Q QUESTIONS TO ASK IF YOUR CHILD IS FEELING ANXIOUS

Q What's causing this?

This won't always be obvious to you or them. Your child might say X is the cause, when really it's Y. This could be because either they're embarrassed to tell you about Y or they don't even understand what's behind their feelings. You might need to tease their worry out of them. If you can't, will they tell another trusted friend or relative?

Q What can you or your child do to remove or reduce the cause of their anxiety?

▶ Sometimes you'll be able to resolve the root cause, e.g. by helping them deal with a bullying or friendship issue.

▶ Some anxieties are based on misunderstandings that you can clear up just by talking. Your child might worry that if they fail their exams, you'll love them less for example. Once you've reassured them this isn't the case, their stress might reduce.

▶ With triggers that are beyond your or your child's control, provide reassurance and perspective. For instance, if your child is worried about terrorism, you can explain that whilst there's a very small risk of being involved in an incident, and that life involves risks, we should still carry on living normally whenever possible.

▶ Don't promise to solve problems that you cannot, as this erodes trust. For example, if a grandparent is seriously ill and your child is worried that they will die, you shouldn't say this won't happen.

Q How can we alleviate the symptoms of their anxiety?

This will obviously vary according to the cause. Sometimes just talking about worries together helps. Ask them to articulate their fears: is the worst thing that can happen really as bad as they believe? How likely is it?

▶ Relaxation techniques, such as simple meditation and deep breathing can help. Even just taking a walk together or a drive – a great, relaxed situation to chat in.

▶ Writing things down can be cathartic. You could suggest your child keeps a diary or, for younger ones, try a 'worry eater' toy (it symbolically gobbles up their worry!).

▶ If your child remains overwhelmed by their feelings and nothing is helping, seek outside help from their GP, school counsellor (where available) or a relevant children's charity. Thankfully there's no longer a stigma to the mental health issues that many young people do deal with, so don't let that stop you gaining support.

MY CHILD SEEMS DEPRESSED

Depression is a mood disorder involving feeling very down all the time and it can affect people of all ages. It's distinct from merely feeling sad for a short spell because it tends to be persistent and all-encompassing.
[source: www.youngminds.org]

Depression can be a reaction to events such as family breakdown, bullying or abuse, and sometimes runs in families, although some people develop depression with no family history or obvious triggers.

IS YOUR CHILD DEPRESSED?

Common symptoms:

persistent sadness

being irritable or grumpy all the time

loss of interest in things they used to enjoy

feeling tired

Other potential symptoms...

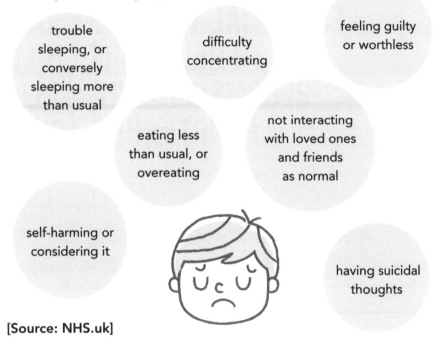

trouble sleeping, or conversely sleeping more than usual

difficulty concentrating

feeling guilty or worthless

eating less than usual, or overeating

not interacting with loved ones and friends as normal

self-harming or considering it

having suicidal thoughts

[Source: NHS.uk]

What you can do

'It's good to talk' – try to gently find out what your child is feeling. If they won't discuss things with you, might they do so with a trusted family friend, relative or teacher?

▶ Listen and take them seriously; no matter how trivial their concerns might seem to grown-up ears, if it's troubling them, it needs addressing.

▶ If you think your child is depressed and needs further help or support, see your GP or speak to their teacher, form tutor or head of pastoral care at school.

ESSENTIAL THINGS NEEDED TO HELP YOUR CHILD BECOME A HAPPY, WELL-FUNCTIONING ADULT

As parents our role is bigger than giving our offspring a happy childhood, it's also to help them become happy, well-functioning adults.

A philosophical mindset: teach them to ask 'why?' And to take a step back, think and question.

Attention: but not too much! Your child should know they matter enormously to you but equally that the world doesn't revolve around them all the time. They need attention to learn, to explore ideas, to build self-esteem and benefit from your guidance.

Praise: a powerful self-esteem booster and motivator but don't overdo it, or praise loses its value: 'don't praise them for breathing'.

Perspective: not something most children are very good at having. When things go wrong help them understand that often situations are not as bad as they initially seem. Provide examples from their own past and yours of how outcomes turned out OK in the end.

A positive role model: children learn from and copy the adults around them.

Firm boundaries: children thrive when they know what is and is not allowed. Set family rules, have appropriate consequences (see Chapter 1, page 11).

Appropriate freedoms: stifled children will struggle with independence and street-wise skills as young adults. Don't wrap them in cotton wool until they're let loose at 18.

Plus the obvious! Love.

Problem-solving skills: guide and direct your child towards solutions, rather than always stepping in on their behalf. The aim: they build the thinking skills and confidence to solve issues for themselves.

Parenting a child who is struggling with mental health issues is stressful so make sure you don't neglect your own well-being and don't blame yourself. Remember too that you aren't alone — support is out there and there's no shame in seeking it or being in this situation.

BUILDING POSITIVE SELF-IMAGE

Where does criticism come from?

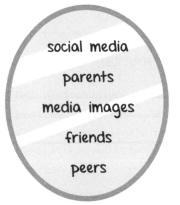

social media

parents

media images

friends

peers

Pre-teens and teens agonising over their appearance is nothing new (many of us did so after all) but, thanks to social media and 'celebrity culture', the intensity of self-scrutiny has deepened and the age it kicks in is now even earlier.

What you can do

Address rather than dismiss body self-criticisms

We all think our kids are beautiful so it's easy to say 'don't be silly' but they might not see the same things as us when they look in the mirror (or at their latest selfie), or have the same benchmarks.

Explain the impact of social media photos

Of course if the majority of photos you see use 'filters', airbrushing or are of surgically-enhanced models and reality TV stars, you're not going to have a realistic view of what 'normal' people look like. Some of the 'before' and 'after', no filters or no make-up shots online are worth looking at together.

Be body positive yourself

Do you complain about your flabby tummy or how you don't like your legs, nose or sticky out ears? Do you discuss other peoples' bodies critically in your child's presence? Children pick up on this. They start to scrutinise themselves in the same way.

Focus on non-physical traits in others, including your children

Try not to mention too often 'you're pretty' or 'you're handsome' or anything similar, as it becomes their defining factor.

Focus on the physical strengths of your bodies

So, yes your child's legs are muscular but that makes them strong. Your own stomach has stretch marks, because it dealt with the wonder of pregnancy.

It's not just a problem for girls

Much of the emphasis on body image in the media relates to girls but boys need help with this too. Keep an eye on their comments and behaviour for warning signs that they've developed unrealistic ideals of their own or female bodies. Are they criticising themselves about aspects of their body that are actually 'normal'?

DEALING WITH GENDER ISSUES

Gender issues are being talked about much more than even a decade ago, whether it's simply avoiding stereotyping (of the 'blue for a boy' type), or something more complex, such as a child who is confused over their identity.

Retailers, nurseries and schools are now less likely to assign playthings to being 'for girls' or 'for boys' and there are now numerous 'gender-neutral' children's clothing lines. Schools are also starting to bring in more flexibility between traditional girl and boy uniforms.

GENDER ISSUES: NEED TO KNOW...

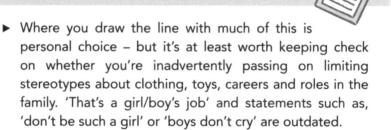

- ▶ Where you draw the line with much of this is personal choice – but it's at least worth keeping check on whether you're inadvertently passing on limiting stereotypes about clothing, toys, careers and roles in the family. 'That's a girl/boy's job' and statements such as, 'don't be such a girl' or 'boys don't cry' are outdated.

- ▶ Some families will go further and favour gender-neutral clothing and names for their young children. Once kids get to school age they are more likely to take the lead on all this themselves, either way.

- ▶ In the pre-teen or teen years, children might particularly experiment with their gender identity, for example wanting to wear the clothing typical of the other gender or change their name. This might (or might not) be a phase – even a form of rebellion or attempt to fit in with a peer group – and will likely pass. If it does continue and your child seems distressed by these issues, seek the advice of your GP, their school counsellor or pastoral care lead. This is much more commonplace these days so, again, there's no need to feel awkward or embarrassed.

What you can do

▶ See if it is a phase or a more permanent issue.

▶ Don't mock your child either way.

▶ If you disagree with what they're doing, state this but don't turn things into a battle of wills. That won't help anyone.

▶ Seek specialist help and support – this is increasingly available. Schools will almost definitely have prior experience of such situations.

MY CHILD IS LYING

Most children go through a stage of experimenting with lying. At some point, when they're toddlers or pre-schoolers, they realise that you won't necessarily know if they did whack little Joshua on the head or not, or that it was them who ate that chocolate cake which was meant to be for Grandma's visit (well, unless they've got half of it smeared around their chin… bit of a giveaway, kids).

We all tell 'white' lies some of the time (how about when your partner asks 'does my bum look big in this' or 'do you like your birthday present?'). Children need to learn when and how lying is acceptable and when it's absolutely not. Sometimes they get in a muddle.

WHY KIDS LIE

- ▶ As a power play or to test boundaries.

- ▶ To avoid getting into trouble.

- ▶ Because they're embarrassed about what they really said or did.

- ▶ To get to do what they want.

- ▶ To garner extra attention (from other children or adults).

What you can do

Understand what's behind the lies if your child fibs regularly

Is there a pattern? When they're embarrassed? Scared? Feeling insecure? If you spot an underlying cause, you can then talk about it.

Call your child's bluff

Where applicable be prepared to double check or call them out on their behaviour but be willing to follow through, so they take you seriously in future – 'Shall I phone Chloe's parents and ask them if that's what really happened?'

Explain the importance of telling the truth

Tell them how it's needed so others trust you and can rely on what you're saying. Give examples. For younger children read stories such as *The Boy Who Cried Wolf*.

Praise honesty

Statements such as, 'I'm not happy that you did X but I'm glad you were at least truthful with me,' encourage truthfulness and doesn't take away from dealing with whatever they have done wrong.

Discuss the difference between positive white lies and unacceptable, negative ones

White lies, such as pretending you like that awful birthday present from Great Aunt Maude, are there to avoid hurting people's feelings. Negative lies erode people's trust and respect. Even fairly young children can start to understand the difference.

Set a good example

We all tell the odd lie but if you persistently do so in front of them, or even get your child to lie on your behalf ('I'm late for school because my baby sister was sick,' when really you all overslept), you'll be normalising lying.

MY CHILD HAS A FEAR OR PHOBIA

Fears are a normal part of childhood and can range from the fairly rational such as dying, war, wasps (is there really anything to like about wasps?) to the bizarre – men with beards and clowns. Our bodies are designed to respond when faced with danger – some people are more sensitive than others, and children can get a shade muddled over what is and isn't a threat. Sometimes there will have been a trigger event – becoming scared of dogs after being barked at by a fierce-looking canine, other times it's caused by an over-active imagination – a fear of the dark perhaps.

What you can do

Take your child's fear seriously

Even if their fear is something that's absurd to you. Saying they're being silly or teasing them isn't going to address what's going on.

Reassure them

If the thing they're scared by isn't actually a threat, reassure them about it. If it is something genuinely dangerous but very rare such as being struck by lightning, then put their fear in perspective and talk about what can be done to limit the chances of it happening. Obviously if they're mid-hysterical freak out, this isn't going to work, so save the calm discussion for later.

Avoid transferring your own fears or phobias

If you jump a mile every time a wasp comes within a 10-foot radius, it's increasing the chances of your son or daughter copying you. If you can't hide your fear, now might be the time to seek help to address it.

Attempt a little desensitisation

By getting them very gently used to something they see as a threat, you might be able to show them that their fears are unfounded.

Is there another issue involved?

Keep in mind that sometimes phobias develop as a symptom of another issue such as anxiety or stress.

If their fear or phobia is getting in the way of everyday life or stopping them enjoying activities, seek help. Talk to your GP who can refer you for specialist support if needed.

STRESS BUSTERS FOR KIDS

- ▶ Get physical – go for a good walk, run about or play some sport together.

- ▶ Meditate – there are apps to help if they don't know how.

- ▶ Talk about it – bottling up feelings is stressful!

- ▶ Watch something funny.

- ▶ Stroke a cat or dog! If you haven't got one, borrow or visit someone else's.

- ▶ Deep breaths – when we're stressed we don't always breath properly.

- ▶ Keep a journal – encourage them to write down the good, bad and ugly of their day – it's cathartic.

- ▶ Find your inner-child and share it: have a pillow or water fight with the kids.

- ▶ Listen to chill-out music during bath time.

- ▶ Let your hair down with them: dance around the kitchen madly.

- ▶ Tell jokes (search online if they don't know any).

- ▶ Do some art – colouring-in perhaps – or crafts.

Remind your child now and then that although they might think absolutely everyone else is happier or more confident or having a far, far better time than they are, we rarely know the truth of others' lives, thoughts or fears. All we see is the window dressing, the edited highlights of what they tell us, what they post on social media... through filters. We only truly know what goes on in our own mind and lives, nobody else's. Encourage your child to focus on themselves rather than making comparisons.

CHAPTER 3

FRIENDS
AND FOES

- ▶ Encouraging healthy friendships
- ▶ What to do when friends fall out
- ▶ Helpful things to say to your child about bullying
- ▶ Reasons (not excuses) why children bully
- ▶ What to do when your child is being bullied
- ▶ How to deal with cyberbullying

- ▶ The subtle impact of social media on children's friendships

- ▶ Ways to bully-proof your child

- ▶ What to do if your child struggles to make friends

- ▶ How to maximise sleep and save your sanity at sleepovers

- ▶ Playdate Q&A

ENCOURAGING HEALTHY FRIENDSHIPS

Some children seem to just naturally be 'good friends' to each other. If yours is having difficulties in their friendships – either not being a true friend themselves or hanging around with children who are letting them down, help your child understand the ingredients that make strong peer bonds.

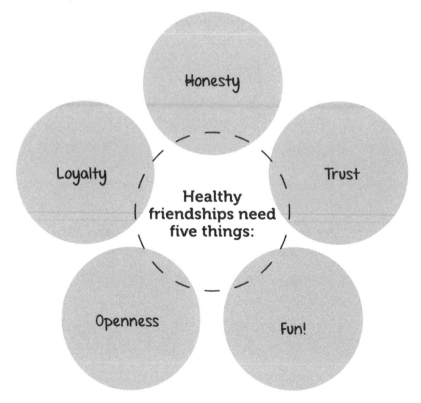

Honesty

Loyalty

Trust

Healthy friendships need five things:

Openness

Fun!

WHAT TO DO WHEN FRIENDS FALL OUT

Your child's come home from school in floods of tears – it's the dreaded friendship fall out...

Younger children in particular fall in and out with friends quicker than you can fathom what's even gone on in that playground squabble. Older kids' friendships tend to be more stable but the problem is that when issues do occur, they have more impact because the fact that relationships are less fluid now, means it's more difficult to replace lost friends.

What you can do

Provide sympathy and reassurance

And a hug... even if you know it'll blow over, it all feels important to your child. That said, if they're in out-of-proportion histrionics, you might want to minimise your response and focus on providing perspective.

Guide your child to solve issues themselves

It's tempting to pile in and mend the friendship like a parent version of a UN Peacekeeper. Yes, you'd love to call the other child's parent and tell them how vile Emily has been or grab Harry and have a word with him about patching things up over the dispute with your child. But try not to. Your child will benefit more from fixing this by themselves but with your guidance and support backing them up. Discuss what they could say and do together and even role play if you have a younger child who might find this a confidence boost.

Help them use these experiences to learn about relationships

Children can learn a lot about relationships via their early friendships. Guide them if you think they're overreacting to something minor that a friend does. Or conversely if they're being too forgiving of someone who is treating them badly, help them see this and stand up for themselves.

Questions to ask your child when they've fallen out with a friend

▶ What do you think your friend feels that made them do or say X?

▶ Is this something you want to solve – do you want to remain friends?

▶ What could you do or say to make this better?

HELPFUL THINGS TO SAY TO YOUR CHILD ABOUT BULLYING

'Whoever is trying to bring you down, is already beneath you.'

'It's not you with a problem, it's the bullies.'

'Not everyone can like you. You will find your kind of people even if it is hard at the moment. It won't always be this way.'

'Don't change who you are just because you think it will make you more popular.'

'Bullies feed on attention – try to not show a reaction.'

'If you wouldn't say it to their face, then don't say it online.'

'Calling someone ugly/fat/stupid won't make you better looking/thinner/cleverer.'

'They can call you a geek but Bill Gates is a geek and look at him...'

REASONS (NOT EXCUSES) WHY CHILDREN BULLY

There can be a number of reasons why your child may be bullying another. It's worth getting to the root cause rather than doling out a punishment straightaway as this won't resolve the real issues at play. They may be bullying for the following reasons:

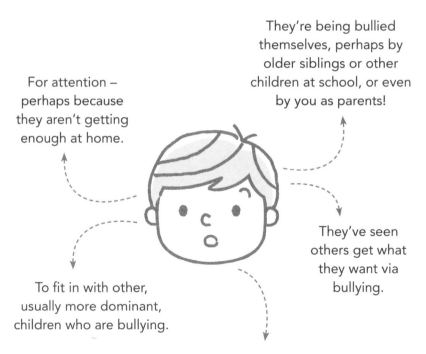

They're being bullied themselves, perhaps by older siblings or other children at school, or even by you as parents!

For attention – perhaps because they aren't getting enough at home.

To fit in with other, usually more dominant, children who are bullying.

They've seen others get what they want via bullying.

All of the above!

When your child is the bully

It can be hard to be honest with yourself and recognise that your child is a bully. It's embarrassing and awkward and you'll probably just wish it wasn't happening. Look out for signs that your child might be bullying others if you get a feeling that it's a possibility:

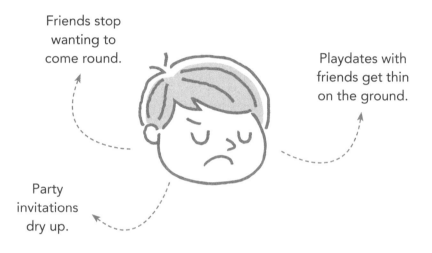

Friends stop wanting to come round.

Playdates with friends get thin on the ground.

Party invitations dry up.

Talk to your child about why they are behaving the way they are and think carefully about which of the underlying causes might apply so you can tackle the issue.

WHAT TO DO WHEN YOUR CHILD IS BEING BULLIED

Bullying is an upsetting part of too many children's lives. It can be emotional, physical or verbal, face-to-face (offline) and online.

The relatively good news is that there is much more awareness and help available now than when we were kids and bullying tends to be taken more seriously by schools.

On the downside, cyberbullying has added a new dimension for this generation of youngsters. It sometimes allows perpetrators to be anonymous, or at least faceless, and means that the bullied have nowhere to escape to as the tormenting follows them home.

Signs your child might be being bullied

	online	offline	both
Unwillingness to go to school			✓
Feeling – or saying they feel – ill in the mornings			✓
Coming home from school with belongings that are damaged or missing		✓	
Generally seeming anxious or depressed			✓

	online	offline	both
Unexplained injuries such as cuts and bruises		✓	
Appearing withdrawn or shy compared to previously			✓
Worsening academic performance			✓
Talking about or feeling suicidal or self-harming			✓
Hiding their phone or tablet or not talking about what they are doing online or checking gadgets more obsessively than normal	✓		

What you can do

Be a shoulder to cry on

Listen, don't dismiss what your child feels as 'not a big deal', or conversely make them talk about it more than they're ready to. If it helps them to open up, suggest they write down what's happened and agree whether you can read what they say or not.

Guide your child to deal with minor issues themselves

If the bullying is relatively minor, suggest ways to respond to it. Your child could try simply ignoring it and avoiding the bullies (though this isn't always possible), pretending they don't care what's being said or using a clever retort.

Avoid approaching the bully's parents

They're rarely going to accept their child's culpability so there is little to be gained. Sometimes doing this could make matters worse if the parents tell their child.

Tackle persistent or severe problems via school

Schools nowadays will usually take bullying seriously. For minor cases get your child to speak to their class teacher or tutor, for more severe bullying, go in yourself. Having your child keep a diary of incidents will be helpful so that teachers can understand the frequency and nature of what's going on.

Bolster your child's self-esteem

Encourage friendships outside of school if your child is being bullied there. Extra-curricular activities such as sports clubs and Scouts or Guides work well for this. Make an extra effort to highlight to your child their positive qualities. Remind them that this is not their fault and is probably more about the bullies' insecurities than their own.

Seek further support

If you're struggling to assist your child or resolve the situation, there's help and advice out there for both parents and children, either from one of the anti-bullying charities (try www.kidscape.org.uk or www.bullying.co.uk) or schools, particularly where they have a counsellor.

HOW TO DEAL WITH CYBERBULLYING

Cyberbullying is any kind of bullying that happens online – it could be via social media, messaging services, email, text, apps or chat rooms. Sometimes it's linked to face-to-face bullying, sometimes not. One in five 13–18 year olds claims they've experienced cyberbullying according to the site www.internetmatters.org – a superb resource on the subject.

What you can do

Talk about cyberbullying with your child

Be aware of new apps kids are using

Take and keep screenshots

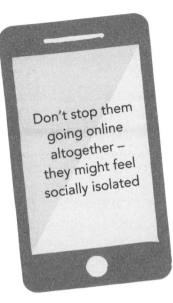

Don't stop them going online altogether – they might feel socially isolated

Consider involving the police (in severe cases)

What your child can do:

- ▶ Not respond to abusive messages

- ▶ Ask friends to remove upsetting comments or images

- ▶ Block the sender and report to the service provider if needed

- ▶ Keep you informed and tell you how they feel

- ▶ Report the issue to their school if the bully is a pupil

THE SUBTLE IMPACT OF SOCIAL MEDIA ON CHILDREN'S FRIENDSHIPS

Social media's impact on children goes beyond overt cyberbullying. It can also be used to exclude, tease and subtly put down other kids, all in new ways that did not exist when we were young. Keep an eye out for some of these situations and agree with your child that you can have access to their gadgets now and then to check what's going on in their online lives, if they're comfortable with that. If they're a shade older and feel they want some privacy, at least keep communicating with them about any issues.

Your child can see what they've been excluded from socially

'They didn't ask me along...'

SHOPPING

**Discussions of who is friends with whom
are very blatantly there for all to see**

**It's easier for kids to brag, and others to feel that
their lives are lacking compared to those of friends**

Popularity is very transparent

'Nobody liked my photo, so I'm not as pretty or popular as them...'

WAYS TO BULLY-PROOF YOUR CHILD

There's no magic way to ensure your child is never a target but there are things you can do to reduce the chances.

Keep channels of communication open with your child

The more willing they are to share experiences of bullying with you, the sooner you might be able to help them nip things in the bud.

Encourage them to be an individual but to fit in with their peers at least somewhat

If your child has quirky and unusual interests and hobbies, it's worth encouraging them to gen up on some of the core topics of conversation among their peers too. Sometimes this is about being aware of the 'in' TV programmes or YouTubers, for others it's about being able to discuss football. It helps them have common ground and build bridges.

Advise them to minimise their reaction to taunts or teasing

Bullies want to trigger a rise out of their targets. Often if they don't get it, they move on. Walking away confidently or having a simple, strong retort can fend them off.

Show them how to walk tall

Demonstrating a confident physical demeanour is another ingredient that can deflect a bully. Show your child how to look physically assertive if needed – by walking tall, looking people in the eye and seeming strong.

Build self-esteem and confidence

Fostering an extra-curricular interest they're good at can help boost confidence and a confident child might feel more able to repel bullies. Drama classes in particular can be effective for this.

Encourage friendships in other scenarios

Non-school friendships can also boost self-esteem and show your child that there are others out there that appreciate them even if those at school don't so much.

WHAT TO DO IF YOUR CHILD STRUGGLES TO MAKE FRIENDS

If your child sits on the playground edge or in the lunch hall all alone, or is left off party invitation lists, it can be heart-wrenching for both of you. Just like adults, some children find it easier to befriend people than others.

What you can do

Consider whether they seem happy with the status quo

Not everyone can be, or wants to be, the life and soul of the party. Some people of all ages are content with their own company or just a very small circle of friends.

Take the initiative

Invite some kids over to promote bonding. If so-called playdates aren't working at home, mix things up – invite another child bowling or to the park instead.

For older children, this starts to get trickier as Mum or Dad can't always get involved but encourage your child to ask some potential friends round. Changing schools can be challenging when it comes to making friends, so this is especially a good time to take the initiative and send some social invitations out.

Encourage non-school friendships

If your child struggles at school, is there scope for friendship building at their extra-curricular activities or via family friends? If your youngster has different interests to classmates, out-of-school activities could be a better source of friendships. Building relationships in another setting could also boost their confidence back at school.

Observe their interactions with other children

Watch how they behave socially. Is there some way they're putting their peers off – perhaps by being shy, aggressive or bossy? If so, talk to them and work out what they could do differently next time. Role play can be beneficial for younger children.

Talk to their teacher

Your child's teacher or form tutor might already have an awareness of any social issues or the personalities and dynamics in the class. There might be another pupil in class who they feel is similar to your child and he or she might be able to encourage things along.

HOW TO MAXIMISE SLEEP AND SAVE YOUR SANITY AT SLEEPOVERS

'Awakeovers' would be a better name for sleepovers given the amount of actual sleep kids tend to get on them. Children seem to love them but they need managing to avoid being a parental headache.

What you can do

Be realistic; the kids probably won't get much sleep...

Don't be under any illusions that because your child and their guests are normally tucked up and asleep by 8 or 9 p.m., that this will be the case on a sleepover. This is all way too exciting for that.

Only schedule sleepovers when there's nothing much going on the day after

It will feel less stressful for you if there's nothing important they need to be fresh and lively for the next day. For this reason, it's sensible to only allow sleepovers at weekends or during school holidays.

Prepare them to sleep by calming things down and giving warnings

Have a more calming activity later in the evening when you want them to settle a bit. Then give the children a half hour warning before it's time to quieten down, and then a further warning a few minutes beforehand. Of course, realistically, this might not work if they are particularly over-excited.

If your efforts to get them to be quiet fail, threaten no further sleepovers for a given amount of time

Keep your threat realistic and be prepared to follow through. This usually gets kids toeing the line.

Keep numbers sensible

Hosting 12 kids for that birthday sleepover might seem like fun but trust me, it really won't be. At least one guest will stay up until 5 a.m. and another will wake at 6 a.m. You will get no sleep.

Have a contingency plan for younger guests or first timers

Agree with their parents that they'll be contactable and vaguely nearby if their child isn't used to sleepovers. Don't be afraid to call the sleepover off and ask them to collect their child if they're very upset.

PLAYDATE Q&A

OK, OK, it's just a modern term for 'having someone round to play' but the classic issues of hosting someone else's child remain. Here's a guide to dealing with some of the most common:

Is it fair to enforce our usual house rules?

Solution: As long as it's something reasonable and you make them aware of it, it's fair to ask visitors to go with the 'our house, our rules' approach. It sends a confusing message to your own children otherwise. Explain the rules to visitors on arrival if needed, give an extra warning for milder misdemeanours but don't be afraid to pull them up if they break rules.

The visiting child is misbehaving – should I tell them off?!

Solution: Dealing with other people's kids when they're up to no good can be a minefield – particularly since they might well go home and complain to their parents about how mean you allegedly were! In case they have different expectations in their family, give them a warning first (unless they've clearly done something very serious) and tone your telling off down a shade.

This visiting child is really out of control. I want to send them home now!

⌐→ **Solution:** In extreme circumstances, absolutely call the other parents to collect their child early (but see below about explaining this to their mum or dad).

The kids are squabbling!

⌐→ **Solution:** Step in and set ground rules, e.g. taking turns, talking respectfully instead of shouting.

They can't find something they both want to do

⌐→ **Solution:** Suggest a more structured activity to bridge the divide if they've little in common. Classic board games or baking something delicious are fairly universally liked. As a last resort, there's always the TV.

The other child has written on my walls/hit my child/ tried to murder the dog – should I tell their parents?

⌐→ **Solution:** It's probably not worth telling them about anything minor – it can sound gripey. For more serious incidents, choose words and tone carefully. Try a 'positive–negative–positive sandwich': say whatever happened after and before two aspects of the visit that were better. So 'she was really enthusiastic about lunch – what a great eater. There was the incident with the nail varnish bottle [cue parent asking what happened...] but on the whole it went well...'

Our children's choice of friends might not be the ones we favour. For younger offspring, you can still influence this somewhat, for example, by making more effort to invite their more favoured friends over. With secondary school age children, who tend to make their own social arrangements, you largely have to accept they pick their own social circle now. Gently voice any specific concerns you hold (a general 'I don't like them' won't work) but bear in mind that if you push back too hard, your child might well simply be drawn further towards the 'undesirables'.

CHAPTER 4

SCHOOL AND
EDUCATION

- ▶ Getting the balance right with pushy parenting
- ▶ Tips to de-hassle homework
- ▶ How to prevent and deal with exam stress
- ▶ Does your child need a tutor?
- ▶ My child hates school

GETTING THE BALANCE RIGHT WITH PUSHY PARENTING

Research shows that being either under-involved or too pushy can be detrimental for our children's learning and academic achievement. Those with under-involved parents tend to achieve relatively poorly at school, whilst at the opposite end of the scale, the so-called 'Tiger parents' (who push their child to excel above all else) can also cause problems too, particularly with anxiety and stress.

Under-involved

- ► Children's achievement versus their potential is low

- ► Little interaction between home and school

- ► Child's well-being is reasonable but long-term prospects might be damaged

Balanced and supportive

► Children achieve well versus their academic potential but get space to 'be children' too

► Relationship between home and school is more likely to be healthy

► Well-being is higher and anxiety lower

Pushy

► Children achieve more academically in the short term but potentially at the cost of well-being – mental health can be compromised by the pressure

► Little or no free time for daydreaming, creativity and 'idle thoughts'

► Parents can be stressed by the need to organise classes and push their child

► Children struggle to be independent learners if they're used to being spoon-fed

► School staff are sometimes antagonised and undermined by pushy parents

► Can damage relationships between parents and children

The middle-ground is healthiest for most children.

Not everyone can be top of the class – focus on your child doing their best and well for them rather than comparing too much to others who might have different strengths and weaknesses. So, for example, you could say 'I was really impressed by how much effort you put into your revision and preparation for the exams', rather than 'it's a shame you didn't get a higher mark'.

TIPS TO DE-HASSLE HOMEWORK

Homework can be a daily headache. Whether your child is still at primary school and has to make an elaborate papier mâché model or is onto calculus, getting them to sit down and get on with it can be quite the challenge.

What you can do

Integrate homework into an after-school routine

If it's always done at a set time, you'll have to nag them (slightly) less to get started. It will just be 'OK, it's 5 p.m., homework time.'

Make sure they have everything they need

Prevent prevarication by ensuring they've got the calculator, dictionary or colouring pencils ready at the start.

Take away distractions

Have a quiet space for homework and consider banning phones or tablets that aren't directly needed to research the task.

Help younger children but remember it is their homework not yours

Primary schoolers in particular might need you to help clarify what they're meant to do or how to get started. That's different to doing the work for them.

Let teachers know if homework is consistently a struggle

Communicate to their teacher if the homework set is often beyond your child's capabilities – they need to know and won't be aware of this if you help too much.

HOW TO PREVENT AND DEAL WITH EXAM STRESS

Some children take exams in their stride, for others they quite literally bring testing times.

What you can do

Encourage downtime as well as revision

All work and no play can make Jack an exhausted boy – as well as a dull one – and too over-tired to do well in the tests anyway. Ensure your child gets a balance of revision, relaxation and rest.

Help them plan their revision

If they're new to taking exams or not very organised, invest a little time helping them plan their studying. Create a timetable, perhaps with 30–45 minute study bursts, interspersed with breaks. Be aware of the time of day when they work best and make sure they have some fun or relaxation planned too.

Make sure they're fed, watered and well-slept

Clearly a decent night's sleep and a good breakfast won't make up for having done no revision but it's still important. Decent hydration, especially for hot summer exam days, is worth keeping an eye on.

Keep perspective

Older children's public exams might genuinely impact their futures, but a younger child's primary school tests won't end up on their CV. Parental exam anxiety can feel contagious but don't allow yourself or your child to get overly stressed even if everyone else is in a tizz.

Look out for signs of stress

Trouble sleeping or eating, being withdrawn or more irritable, can be signs your child is anxious about exams. Talk to them in the first instance about how they feel and reassure them. If their stress is severe, speak to their school about it.

Remind them it's doing their best that matters

Of course it's nice to do well in exams but if your child has done their best, there's little more that you can ask for.

DOES YOUR CHILD NEED A TUTOR?

In some areas, it can feel like everybody else's child is getting tutored; it's become 'the done thing'. But it's an expensive and time-consuming business that adds workload for your child – it isn't just the tutoring session but the related homework they'll have to do. Before making this commitment, even if it's the norm for local kids, it's wise to ask whether *your* child really needs a tutor.

Scenarios where a tutor can help...

'She's struggling with a particular aspect of her work and some individual tuition will give her a confidence boost.'

'He missed a few weeks of school through illness and is finding it tough to catch up.'

'She's a genuinely bright girl but her primary school doesn't prepare for selective schools' 11+ exams... I want her to go in feeling confident and to level the playing field as most children are tutored before the tests.'

'My son needs some extra support but I can't work with him as my first language isn't English and I can't provide the input he needs.'

Proceed with caution...

'I want her to get into the top maths set/group/be top of the class no matter what!'

'The grammar school is going to be a real stretch for him to get into but if we really go for it with the tutor he might scrape in... and if he struggles once there, well we can keep tutoring...'

'She's only in year two but everyone is being tutored in her class already and if we don't, I think she'll be left behind...'

We all want our children to do well and be successful but should that be at the cost of their childhood and general well-being? Don't be afraid to go against the modern grain of tutoring, endless classes or pressure and take an approach to learning that's right for your child and what *you* want for them. Do remember that time to play, to be imaginative and have idle thoughts, or even 'being bored' for a bit is as valuable or more so than that extra musical instrument or maths tuition when they're already doing perfectly well.

MY CHILD HATES SCHOOL

Not every child skips enthusiastically into their classroom every day. Since school is a significant part of childhood it can be deeply stressful if they don't actually like going.

What you can do

Keep calm

Of course it's tricky and tiring if you're having to practically drag your child to school each day but if they start to associate mornings with being told off, or pressured, it could add to their anxieties. Not easy but try to keep your approach firm but reassuring and relaxed.

Sit tight – it might be a phase

It's not uncommon for kids to go through a spell when they're not happy to go to school. Sometimes this sorts itself out within a few days or weeks.

Make it clear that school is not a choice

If you're strongly suspicious that your child is 'trying it on' to get a few days off, stand firm and let them know that school is non-negotiable – by law they have to go (assuming home schooling isn't a longer term option of course).

Don't let fake illnesses become a headache

Children who want to get out of school are masters at creating fake maladies. For parents it can be difficult to decipher whether they're crying wolf or actually ill. Your best bet: threaten a trip or a phone call to the doctor's. This will probably see them suddenly perk up. Be prepared to actually follow through if needed.

Think about underlying causes

Talk to your child about exactly why they're not keen on school. Do this at a time when everyone is calm – not mid-strop at 8 a.m. when they're running late. Bullying or friendship problems, boredom, learning difficulties or a poor relationship with a teacher can all trigger school aversion, as can issues in their home life. Understanding the cause will help you find solutions.

Discuss the situation with school

Approach their teacher or tutor to talk about the problem – can they shed light on any relevant incidents at school for example? Ideally come up with an action plan as a home–school team.

Still struggling?

In more severe and persistent cases, approach your GP who can refer you for further help if needed.

Relationships between school and parents can sometimes be fraught. Try to focus on the fact that the teachers tend to be experts in education and you're the expert in your child but that both of you can have useful perspectives on the other's area. The best outcomes for children happen when parents and teachers work as a team to solve any problems.

CHAPTER 5

FOOD AND
MEALS

- ▶ My child won't try new foods
- ▶ Ingredients to make fussy eater mealtimes more palatable
- ▶ How to help ensure your child's weight is healthy
- ▶ My child has become vegetarian or carnivore
- ▶ How to limit snacks and junk food

It might not make you feel much better when you're scraping another rejected meal into the bin but children's fussy eating might actually be related to a smart survival instinct; they would have avoided new foods 'in the wild' because the unknown could be harmful.

Another theory is that some children have more sensitive taste buds than other's and are less able to enjoy or even tolerate stronger tastes.

Survival instinct, sensitive taste buds or plain wilfulness... it's irritating all the same.

MY CHILD WON'T TRY NEW FOODS

In a world of chicken nuggets and smiley potato faces, it *is* still possible to instil a love of good, healthy – even adventurous – food in children, if we raise our expectations and theirs.

What you can do

Encourage rather than pressure or force

Pleading or begging for your child to 'just try it' is unlikely to persuade them to do so and can have the opposite effect if they feel overly pressured. Studies have shown that if children are offered two foods and are told which one of them to eat, they'll choose the other. So, demanding they 'eat their greens' isn't the way to get them to actually do it.

Talk positively about the food you want them to eat

Get eating and appreciating it yourself. They might just sit and stare at you as you declare 'mmmm this broccoli is lovely and fresh tasting' but it's worth a go. With younger children try reverse psychology of 'this might be a bit grown up for you... but have some if you want...' most children love the idea of anything 'grown-up'.

Have a rule of 'no saying you don't like it if you've never tried it'

Remind them that they had to try everything once. If they'd refused to taste ice cream or chocolate the first time, and claimed they didn't like it, imagine what they'd have missed out on.

Praise the trying not the liking

If they do taste a food, praise them for giving it a go, not necessarily for liking it.

Let them know there's no pressure if they don't want to eat it all

If your child tries something and genuinely dislikes it, explain you'll accept that and they won't have to eat a full portion. But they must at least taste it with an open mind. This takes the pressure away.

Involve them in what's being served

Involve your child in cooking or growing veg, and provide an edited selection of dinners they can help you pick from (but you're happy with too), so they feel they're getting some choice in meals dished up.

Build links between foods they like and new ones

Explain similarities between foods they eat already and new ideas – so meatballs are just different-shaped burgers for example. Sweet potato wedges are similar to chips.

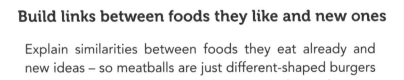

Keep trying

Just because your child hasn't enjoyed a particular food so far doesn't mean they never will. As our taste buds mature, we can start appreciating a food we didn't when younger. Additionally, studies show that the more a child tastes a particular food, the more they might begin to accept it, so keep offering it.

Use dining out as an opportunity to introduce different dishes

If you're eating out and having something more adventurous, encourage your child to try a bit of your food. Buffets are also brilliant for this, as you can take a little of something new without having to order a whole meal of it.

Say no to nuggets!

As a society we seem to have ended up with low expectations of what children will eat; conditioned to think that we need to be rustling up smiley face potato waffles, or grabbing cartoon-covered yogurt pots to fill their tummies. As if they can't just eat normal food. Look at the average restaurant 'kids' menu' – a bland and predictable list of nuggets, pizza, burger and pasta. But children don't need special novelty 'kiddy food' – sometimes they want it, sometimes it does no harm but don't let it become their default.

INGREDIENTS TO MAKE FUSSY EATER MEALTIMES MORE PALATABLE

Eat the same as a family – no separate 'kiddy food'

Keep portion sizes smaller if a child isn't keen on what's dished up – it'll be less overwhelming. Or let them serve themselves so they can gauge how much to try (as long as that isn't none…)

No offering more appealing alternatives if a meal is rejected

Limit the efforts you put into cooking – less annoying if they won't eat it

Be realistic – nobody of any age likes everything

Allow a limited food veto – agree you won't serve a few of their most hated foods

Remind them we can't only eat our 'favourite foods' all the time – sometimes we have to have meals that are just 'OK'.

HOW TO HELP ENSURE YOUR CHILD'S WEIGHT IS HEALTHY

There's much talk of children's weight in the media and in healthcare – with an obesity crisis at one end of the scale (excuse the pun) and pressure to be thin at the other. Between the ages of two and 15, 28 per cent of children are overweight or obese (Office for National Statistics ONS).

What you can do

Never force your child to 'clear their plate'

The old-fashioned approach of making sure kids eat everything served doesn't help them learn to regulate their appetite and recognise when they're full. Help them get a feel for when they've eaten enough.

Look at your own dietary example

Are you setting a good example or skipping meals, scoffing chocolate bars or constantly calorie counting in front of your family?

Try subtle changes

Putting your child on an overt diet can make food into a bigger issue than it needs be and can cause body image hang-ups (see page 45). If they're a bit under- or over-weight, initially try adjusting their meals and snacks to add or remove calories. For teenagers, discuss healthier choices that they can make outside of the home, explaining their impact.

See your GP about more serious weight concerns

If dietary adjustments aren't making a difference, seek your GP's advice.

How to calculate BMI for children

Underweight, <5%   Healthy, 5-84%   Overweight, 85-94%   **Obese, 95% +**

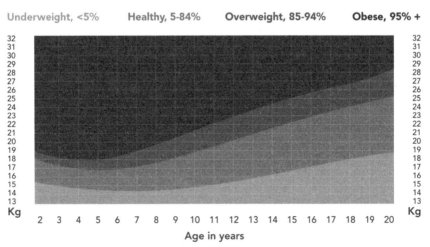

Age in years

This table is intended as a guide only. Please consult a health professional if you have any health or weight concerns about your child.

MY CHILD HAS BECOME VEGETARIAN OR CARNIVORE

It's not at all unusual for children to go against the family grain on whether they eat meat or not. If yours decides they want to be vegetarian or to turn carnivorous (if you're a vegetarian family) when you aren't, don't panic...

What you can do

Discuss don't dismiss

Yes, it's going to be inconvenient for meals and might go against your beliefs but at least find out why your child wants to change their diet. Is it about not wanting to eat animals? Health concerns? Peer pressure? Explain the pros and cons of making the changes they have in mind.

Accept it is their choice

Once you've discussed the issue and informed them about what they're doing, you can't force them to eat meat or to be vegetarian and will need to go with their decision.

Let them try their new diet. They might well change their mind as soon as they get the whiff of their first missed bacon sandwich or realise they aren't so keen on roast dinners after all.

Explain any nutritional issues

Ensure they start to understand that if they're no longer eating meat, they should have other sources of iron and protein in their diet. If they've turned carnivorous, talk about limiting red and processed meats in line with official guidance.

Get them to muck in with cooking more

Depending on their age and skills, if your child wants to go against the family diet, encourage them to make their own food. Suggest they research how you can adapt meals to cater for both meat- and non-meat eaters, such as veggie sausages and meat ones with mash.

HOW TO LIMIT SNACKS AND JUNK FOOD

Many a child would consume a diet solely consisting of chocolate and fast food if allowed. How can you ensure they have a healthy diet without taking away the joy of the occasional piece of cake?

What you can do

Balance don't ban

Scoffing a piece of cake at a birthday party or raiding the freshly-baked biscuits is surely a wondrous part of childhood. To take that away can make goodies all the more alluring. It also does nothing to help children learn the self-regulation they'll need when they grow up and you're no longer there to ban 'naughty' food.

But don't allow junk to be their 'normal'

Turning a blind eye to occasional indulgence is one thing but having a constant supply of junk and sugary treats is clearly a health issue. The easiest way to manage what they eat at home is to not buy too much junk food in the first place.

Consider a junk food night once a week

Some families find it works well to 'ring-fence' less healthy foods by having a weekly 'junk night' with takeaway and ice cream or similar. Not only does everyone get to let their dietary hair down, but it's also a good opportunity to talk about the pros and cons of this sort of food.

Tackle other regular carers if they're allowing too much unhealthy food

If other people care for your child regularly – be it grandparents, a babysitter or ex-partner – and are letting them eat endless junk, it can undermine your own efforts. If it's just occasional, you might have to turn a blind eye, but if they look after your children often, it could be time for a diplomatic chat and some ground rules.

Healthier food swaps... with realistic kid appeal

Let's face it, your children are not going to buy the idea that they should drop the chocolate bar and devour the plain rice cakes, so try these more realistic healthier swaps instead...

Burger and fries (fried)	Oven-baked fish and oven chips
Sugary drinks	Unsweetened yogurt and berry milkshake
Crisps	Pitta chips or popcorn (as long as it isn't too sugar-loaded)
Cake	Granola bars with honey and nuts
Cola drinks	Fizzy water with a squeeze of fruit?
Sugary cereal	Porridge or pancakes with fruit puree

How much sugar is too much?

Excess sugar intake is a big issue for children – recent research suggests our focus should be on reducing this, whereas in the last few decades the emphasis has been about fat. A balanced diet keeps an eye on both these food groups to avoid excesses.

How much sugar is too much per day?

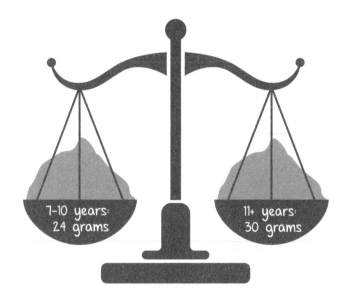

7-10 years:
24 grams

11+ years:
30 grams

[source NHS.uk]

CHAPTER 6

GROWING-UP
ISSUES

- ▶ Children's independence: is the world a more dangerous place to grow up in?

- ▶ Dos and don'ts: leaving your child home alone

- ▶ Dos and don'ts: allowing your child to go out alone

- ▶ You want to wear what?! (clothing battles)

- ▶ My child is swearing

- ▶ Dos and don'ts: how to talk about sex

- ▶ How to talk about drugs

Many of us struggle with balancing our protective instincts, in what we perceive to be a more dangerous world, with allowing our offspring to build all-important independence. But by encouraging appropriate independence, our children:

- learn to be street-wise

- build self-esteem

- feel more trusted.

Remember that your child moving from being dependent to independent is a natural journey that they need to take.

CHILDREN'S INDEPENDENCE: IS THE WORLD A MORE DANGEROUS PLACE TO GROW UP IN?

We perceive the world to be a lot scarier than when we were children but are we wearing rose-tinted specs when we think this?

CHILD SAFETY FACTS: THEN VERSUS NOW

▶ The number of child deaths per year was an average of just over 2,700 in the 1980s in England and Wales. This includes deaths due to illnesses, accidents and crimes. By the first part of the 2010s the average was just over 1,000 per annum. Clearly every one of those is a tragic loss but that's a significant decline.

▶ Child homicides (murder, manslaughter and infanticide) in the UK in 2016 were at the lowest rate since relevant records began in 1972 [ONS].

▶ The number of children dying in road traffic accidents is considerably lower too [ONS].

Despite such statistics, it's hard to tell if there really are fewer threats to our children, as this could be due to today's young being much more supervised than previous generations. The fact is though, the chances of something catastrophic happening to your child are mercifully low and we need to keep this in perspective when faced with alarming 24/7 news coverage.

Going it alone: the law

▶ There are currently no laws in the UK about the age at which children are allowed to go out or stay at home without adult supervision.

▶ It's left to parents to decide what is appropriate since a blanket law doesn't account for different variables, such as an individual child's maturity or the nature of the place they're being left at or are going to.

▶ Parents can however be prosecuted for neglect if their child is left 'in a manner likely to cause unnecessary suffering or injury to health'. So if something goes wrong, you would be held to scrutiny.

▶ Clearly leaving a toddler 'home alone' is never appropriate, whilst equally teenagers are fine for a few hours in the daytime. In between there are grey areas.

▶ The charity NSPCC's guidance suggests children under 16 should not be left overnight and under 12s might lack the maturity to deal with an emergency so should only be left for short periods in the day at most.

DOs AND DON'Ts: LEAVING YOUR CHILD HOME ALONE

Towards the end of primary school, most children are mature enough to cope with at least a short spell at home alone, provided they feel comfortable with this.

DO

1. Start with short periods initially – perhaps twenty minutes whilst you nip to the local shop or walk the dog round the block. Build up over time.

2. Make sure they know what to do in an emergency such as a fire or power cut. If they wouldn't cope with this reasonably well, they probably aren't ready to be left.

3. The first few times, if you have a trusted neighbour, let them know your child is home alone and ask them to be on call if there's an issue.

4. Have clear rules on not answering the door or phone and not cooking. If you do let your child answer the phone they shouldn't tell callers they are alone – instead they could say 'Mum/Dad is busy but they'll call you back'.

5. Tell your child when you'll be back, leave your phone number written out clearly and advise on how to contact

someone else appropriate if they can't call you and need urgent help. If you're delayed returning, let your child know how you'll update them.

6. Leave the phone in a set place so they can find it easily.

DON'T

1. Expect your child to be responsible for much younger siblings if they themselves are under 14 years old.

2. Venture too far the first few times in case there's a problem.

3. Force them to stay at home alone if they don't feel confident to do so.

DOs AND DON'Ts: ALLOWING YOUR CHILD TO GO OUT ALONE

Your protective instincts are pushing you to keep your child wrapped in cotton wool until they're 18... or maybe 45... but at the same time you know they need some freedom as they get older. How can you get that balance right?

DO

1. Assess what is sensible for *your* child – that might be different to everyone else's. Yours might be more or less sensible or street-wise than their peers.

2. Consider the specific risks of where you live – is there a hard-to-cross road or a lot of crime?

1. Set clear rules with the three Ws – *Who* are they going with? *Where* are they allowed to go? *When* must they be back? Make sure your child understands they must check with you if there are any changes to arrangements.

2. Use technology – mobile phones allow you to keep in touch but also to track where your child is. It sounds a bit Big Brother but it's sensible, particularly for initial solo adventures.

3. Remind them of emergency contact details – how to call you or another family member if something goes wrong.

4. Look at other opportunities for independence if they're limited near home. If you can't let them loose much where you live, is there more scope for freedom when visiting grandparents or while you're on holiday?

5. Do a trial run of future independent outings with you nearby – perhaps they could walk on ahead to school or go to a cafe with a friend whilst you shop in the vicinity.

DON'T

1. Dwell on the risks too much… yes occasionally dreadful things happen but we hear about those and remember them, not the many, many thousands of children who are fine.

2. Throw your child in at the deep end. Start with small steps towards independence and build up – initially just walking to the corner shop or postbox, rather than a full-blown shopping mall trip.

3. Scare them about what might happen or pass your anxieties on but do talk about scenarios they may face and what to do, e.g. a stranger approaches them or they get lost. Remind them of road safety rules now and then, especially the modern scourge of looking at phones when crossing roads.

YOU WANT TO WEAR WHAT?! (CLOTHING BATTLES)

From denim in the Swinging Sixties to the perennial problem of the 'skirt that looks more like a belt', parents and kids have long argued about what appropriate attire is.

Teenagers particularly look to clothing and image to at best distance themselves from their parents, or at worst to rile them. Wearing things parents don't approve of goes with the territory. If this is their way of rebelling and building identity, count your blessings – it's probably just a phase.

What you can do

If it's just that you don't like the style of their outfit

Within reason children want and need to develop and express their individuality and self-image. If you don't think the green T-shirt goes with the purple shorts, or get irritated that they wear sunglasses inside, leave them be and save your battles for other problems. It's tempting to feel that what they wear reflects badly on you but your kids are not an extension of your style.

However, if their outfit is offensive or inappropriate... help them to understand the impression they're giving

First up, point out the impression their outfit might give others – people genuinely do make judgments based on appearance and your child simply might not realise their image is going to be viewed negatively.

Consider why they're dressing the way they are

Is it to fit in? To attract boys or girls? Are they feeling insecure about themselves? Or is it to provoke you? Trying to understand this can help shape your reaction.

I'm wearing this because...

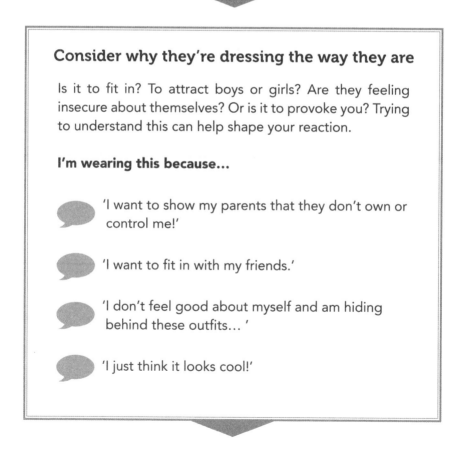

'I want to show my parents that they don't own or control me!'

'I want to fit in with my friends.'

'I don't feel good about myself and am hiding behind these outfits... '

'I just think it looks cool!'

Look for compromises

Could your daughter wear the short skirt with opaque tights or leggings? Stick with the top but wear it with more conservative 'bottoms'? Or you could allow the sweatshirt or T-shirt with the (arguably) offensive slogan when they're off out meeting their friends, but not when they're seeing the grandparents.

Send them shopping with someone else

If your son or daughter doesn't want to listen to your sartorial guidance anymore, can they be influenced in their clothing choices and look by a relative or friend one step away?

MY CHILD IS SWEARING

Way back when, if we uttered so much as a 'damn' as children – or up to the age of about 25 in the case of my mum and dad's rules – our parents would threaten us with a soap and water mouthwash. Times have certainly changed. Society now sees milder swearwords as more acceptable – albeit not usually from the mouths of babes. Whilst you still probably don't want your seven-year-old shouting the f-word in front of the vicar, head teacher or Great Aunt Jemima, things are less clear-cut for older children and milder swearwords.

What you can do

Consider providing younger children with a pretend 'swear' word

The act of 'swearing' has been shown to be beneficial – it can relieve stress, enhance pain-resistance and help frustrations dissipate. Young children can get the upsides without offending Granny, via a 'proxy' swearword – it could be the traditional choice of 'sugar'.

Set the example

If you're forever effing and blinding, your kids will copy you. It's how they learnt to talk in the first place after all...

Older children and teens won't 'buy' the idea that you can swear and they can't

In previous generations, adults were accepted as living by different rules to children. They could say 'I'm an adult so can swear but you can't'. Like it or not, modern kids don't really accept this. So don't swear in front of them and expect them not to do so. To be fair it doesn't really make much sense that adults would be allowed and not children.

Once they can discern that there's a 'time and place' consider easing restrictions

By relaxing rules as your children get older, you'll allow swearing to be less taboo and take away some of its power to shock. The key is to do this only when they can discern when it is (relatively) OK to swear and when it isn't.

Before the age of seven, they're unlikely to be able to judge this. Most children can do so at ten or 11 – the move to secondary school can be a good watershed for relaxing rules somewhat. Explain the sort of words you will and

will not allow and give examples of the types of occasions they're permitted, e.g. no swearing in front of others, especially younger children or older relatives who tend to be more conservative about such matters.

DOs AND DON'Ts: HOW TO TALK ABOUT SEX

We might live in relatively liberal times but talking about sex with our children can still make most of us feel at least a shade awkward. Being able to discuss sex in an open and friendly manner is crucial towards keeping communication going about this through the teenage years.

Do

▶ **Talk about it** – if you don't, your child could pick up misinformation from their peers or might search online for answers where material might be inappropriate or inaccurate.

▶ **Raise the subject** – if they haven't asked you about sex by the last year or so of primary school, this is a good time to start a dialogue. This coincides with when most schools introduce the subject as part of their 'personal, social and health education' (PSHE) lessons.

▶ **Be matter of fact but friendly in your tone** – research has shown that children whose parents discussed sex in a warm and friendly manner when they were young were less likely to engage in sexual activity in secondary school and more likely to use contraception when they did, versus those whose parents used a contentious tone.

▶ **Use books if you feel awkward** – these can be an ice breaker and support discussion rather than replacing it. Give your child a decent, age-appropriate book on puberty and sex but make it clear you are there to answer their questions afterwards if you don't read it together.

▶ **Introduce discussion of safe sex in the early secondary school years** – schools should cover this but mention it before your child seems to be at the stage of starting to be sexually active.

Don't

▶ **Use too many euphemisms for body parts** – children just find them confusing. Even if you've grown up saying 'front bottom' or 'twinky' (!), it really is preferable to use anatomically correct names.

▶ **Dodge their questions** – if they're old enough to ask, they're old enough to receive an (age-appropriate) answer.

▶ **Be embarrassed** – be careful not to pass on the idea that sex is something awkward or embarrassing – yes it's personal but it's also a natural human function.

HOW TO TALK ABOUT DRUGS

Most teenagers will be offered drugs at some stage, so your best bet is to arm them with information and ensure they know they can come to you to discuss things.

Tips for talking about drugs

- ▶ Use TV programmes and films as starting points for a dialogue on drugs. It will seem more natural if you're struggling to raise the topic in a relaxed way.

- ▶ Make sure your child is aware of the risks of different types of drugs – not just the physical and mental effects, but increasing their exposure to harm and exploitation.

- ▶ Encourage open conversation about drugs. Start introducing discussion during the pre-teen years – pupils at secondary schools will usually have some awareness of issues from sessions at school.

- ▶ Do your homework on what's out there and check on current terminology (try the website www.talktofrank.com for this and also for general advice on the subject), so that you're better able to spot any mentions of narcotics by your child online or when they're with their friends.

- ▶ Keep an eye on their friendship groups – encourage your teenager to have their friends round so you can meet them.

▶ Be realistic rather than alarmist in your advice – 'cannabis can kill you' is over-the-top, for example, and highlighting realistic negatives will be more likely to sink in.

Strategies to try if your teen won't listen to your advice on risky behaviour

▶ Ask another adult they respect and trust to talk to them instead (as long as you aren't breaching your child's confidence).

▶ Use a film, book, TV programme, news story or vlog as a talking point or to actually make the point – you might not need to add anything yourself to get the message across…

▶ Speak to their school to find out if their tutor can discuss the problem with them or could arrange a speaker to come in if the issue is something commonplace.

Difficult conversations – about sex, drugs, early relationships – are often easier when there's something else going on as it reduces the intensity. If you're driving in the car with your child sometimes taking away the face-to-face element can make awkward subjects less difficult to broach – plus they can't avoid the conversation as they're strapped into a car with you!

CHAPTER 7

SCREEN
TIME

▶ Ways to reduce your family's screen use

▶ Is your child really addicted to screens?

▶ When should you get your child their own mobile phone?

▶ Dealing with social media issues

▶ How to keep your child safe online

▶ Sexting – keeping your teen safe

▶ Positive screen-time activities

" Screens are part of all our lives now – it's when they become life itself that we have a problem. "

WAYS TO REDUCE YOUR FAMILY'S SCREEN USE

Create and enforce 'family screen rules'. Stick them on the fridge! Everyone has to follow the rules unless stated otherwise – including parents!

Here are a few suggestions:

- No screen use during meals or when visitors are over.

- No gadgets in bedrooms for the last hour before bed (screen glare can inhibit sleep).

- Gadgets are to be charged downstairs (to prevent 'secret' use after bedtime).

- A time limit of an hour a day for younger children (under sevens).

- No (recreational) gadget use until after homework or chores are done.

Set the example

Children learn from the adults around them – if you're checking the football scores during dinner or constantly scrolling through social media feeds... guess what your kids will perceive as normal?

Consider a digital detox

It'll show them they can still have fun offline and you'll all benefit from uninterrupted family time. Detox for a short spell every week, perhaps Sunday afternoons or a whole weekend occasionally.

Hold off on buying them their own gadgets or allowing social media for as long as possible

Ignore pleas of 'everyone at school has... an iPhone 43 or "Instateen" account' – they probably don't and 'everyone' isn't your child anyway.

Don't demonise screen time

It's unwise to make it a 'bogeyman' you battle your kids over. Explain to them that you accept that screens are part of their lives – all of our lives in fact – and have benefits but that you expect sensible usage. Teach them that there's a time and place.

But be aware – as a family – of its downsides

We all need human interaction more than another TV programme or spell on that app. Evidence shows that too much screen time hampers inter-personal skills and is associated with other issues such as poor sleep and obesity.

For older children: think about what they're doing not just *how much*

It used to be that a set limit worked for older kids too but now they might well need to be online to do homework. Not all screen time is equal; compare using an educational website versus mindless gaming. At this age it's about a healthy relationship with tech rather than fixed time limits.

Use the primary school years to educate your child about safe internet usage whilst you can still be involved

Shoulder surf as much as you can in the primary school phase, and for when you can't, have robust parental control software or settings. (See page 149.)

Secondary-school-age offspring are usually out and about with a phone; you'll have less control

Until the mid-teens, have a rule that you can do spot checks of their gadgets – you're (probably) the one paying the bills after all. This way you can monitor what they're up to online (although canny kids will often delete incriminating evidence) and discuss any issues. Aim to keep channels of communication as open as possible so that your child does not feel their privacy is being compromised.

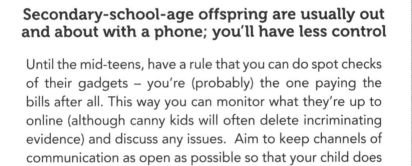

IS YOUR CHILD REALLY ADDICTED TO SCREENS?

A lot of parents declare 'my child is *addicted* to screens...' but in reality, most children are merely a shade over-enthusiastic and not actual addicts, although it does happen.

Signs of true addiction which mean you might need to get outside help include:

- ▶ Preferring screens to people or activities they previously enjoyed (beyond normal teen temperamental behaviour or flightiness of some younger kids!).

- ▶ Behaving badly when you ask them to switch off to do something reasonable, or having a meltdown on a regular basis.

- ▶ Exhibiting classic withdrawal symptoms (anxiety being a key one), when they can't get their screen 'fix'.

- ▶ Lying about screen usage.

- ▶ Significant decline in school performance.

- ▶ Trouble sleeping, or staying up all night to use their gadget.

If you've tried imposing firmer rules and detoxing to no avail, then speak to your GP about this. If needed they can refer you on for specialist support.

WHEN SHOULD YOU GET YOUR CHILD THEIR OWN MOBILE PHONE?

It will make life less complicated if younger children don't have their own gadgets – it's easier to take shared ones away and to police what they are doing on them. Delay getting your child a phone as long as possible.

Questions to help you decide

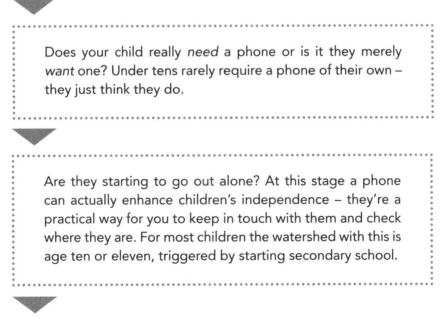

Does your child really *need* a phone or is it they merely *want* one? Under tens rarely require a phone of their own – they just think they do.

Are they starting to go out alone? At this stage a phone can actually enhance children's independence – they're a practical way for you to keep in touch with them and check where they are. For most children the watershed with this is age ten or eleven, triggered by starting secondary school.

Are there any other circumstances meaning a phone might be genuinely useful? For example, in a separated family when they're with their other parent and you want to speak to them directly.

If you do decide to get them a phone, stick with an oldish model initially (yes they will complain...) because it will be less 'stealable' and less of an issue if it gets lost or broken. Upgrade later if they prove they can be sensible. Consider a 'brick' or 'dumb' phone initially, not a smartphone.

DEALING WITH SOCIAL MEDIA ISSUES

Research shows that the more time children chat on social media, the less happy they are. That said, excluding teens from sites such as Facebook, Instagram etc. altogether can in turn hamper their friendships.

Should you let your child have a social media account?

▶ Have they reached the minimum age specified by the app or service provider (usually 13)? We know in the real world not everyone sticks with this though…

▶ If you say no will your child be excluded socially from their friends in any meaningful way? Is 'everyone in the class' genuinely on that app or is your child just saying so? Ask another parent what sort of thing is posted if their child participates.

▶ Are they sensible enough to understand the world of social media and the related cyber safety issues?

▶ Have you discussed online bullying (see page 72)?

▶ Does the app or site have settings to filter who can see posts – can it be set so only their close friends can view them?

TIP: Initially, use social media sites side-by-side with your child if possible, so you can teach them safe and sensible usage and discuss any issues. Then, until they're mature enough to use them unsupervised, transition to still having access to their account(s), so you can monitor posts and messages.

HOW TO KEEP YOUR CHILD SAFE ONLINE

Knowing how to keep our offspring safe online can be especially challenging given it involves apps and products we as parents don't necessarily use or even understand. As soon as we get the hang of the latest app, our kids might well have moved onto the next big trend. Fortunately, many of the principles of cyber-safety apply across the board.

What you can do

Teach them that things are not always as they seem online

People online are not always who they say they are. They should never post their location, personal information or photos unless they are completely sure of who they are talking to. Without being alarmist, give them some examples of problems that could arise. Ask them to *always* check with you before giving out any information.

Explain they should screenshot anything upsetting or suspicious as evidence

Show them how to take a screenshot on their laptop, phone or tablet if they don't already know.

Talk about how 'what goes online stays online'

Possibly forever, for future employers and partners to see. Suggest your child keeps in mind the 'grandma rule' – if you wouldn't want your grandma to see it, don't post it!

Make it clear that they can always talk to you about their concerns

Let your child know that they can and should tell you about anything they've encountered online that's worried or upset them and that they needn't be embarrassed.

Add parental controls on all gadgets your children use

Set up parental controls but don't rely entirely on them – particularly for younger children keep an eye on what they're accessing online to check its appropriateness.

SEXTING: KEEPING YOUR TEEN SAFE

The landscape of early sexual experiences has changed and sexting and the sharing of images is now part of many teens' experimentation with sex. Understandably it worries parents greatly.

What you can do

Explain that sending sexually explicit imagery of a child is illegal

Even if the person doing the sharing is a child. Even if the image is of themselves, or if the other person gave permission. It's against the law.

Remember that 'grandma rule'

If they wouldn't want their grandma seeing an image, then don't press send.

Make it clear that 'what goes online, stays online... forever'

They might not be concerned about their 'digital profile' now, but will probably be one day, e.g. when applying for jobs. Even if they delete that image or post on Snapchat, someone else can 'screenshot' and share.

Explain that even if you trust someone now, relationships can change

Your child might trust their boyfriend, girlfriend or friend they send an explicit image or message to now, but relationships and friendships can deteriorate. No one can assume images will stay private to the person they shared them with now or in future. So 'don't send it if you don't want everyone else seeing it'.

Keep a dialogue going...

Let your teen know that you just want them to be safe and they can talk to you about any concerns with their internet use, without embarrassment or fear of getting in trouble.

POSITIVE SCREEN-TIME ACTIVITIES

Screen time for our children is so often demonised but amidst the aggressive video games, the cyber bullying and inappropriate material grabbing the 'moral panic' headlines, there are amazing, positive things our kids can do on gadgets.

Here are a few ideas:

▶ Learn the names of the constellations with a star gazing app.

▶ Learn a language with one of the interactive, multimedia sites or apps.

▶ Pick up a musical instrument – there are lots of tutorials on YouTube including videos for simpler instruments such as the harmonica or ukulele.

▶ Begin a blog. Older children with a strong interest will enjoy sharing their thoughts on whatever they're into with the world. It could be on anything from sport to cookery.

▶ Work their grey matter with a brain training app.

▶ Boost their school work with an app that makes maths or English more fun.

▶ Encourage reading – e-readers have lots of benefits from an on-board e-dictionary, the ability to change the font size and the chance to download the next book in a series instantly.

▶ Get weather savvy: www.lightningmaps.org plots local lightning strikes in almost real time, whilst www.uksnow. com maps snow depth.

▶ Keep in touch with distant relatives more easily – via Facetime, Skype and email.

Social media only lets us see the glossy side of others' lives – the edited highlights, with filters on top. This can leave children with unrealistic expectations of how exciting everyone else's worlds are. Discuss this so you can provide perspective.

CHAPTER 8

FAMILY
RELATIONSHIPS

- ▶ Encouraging good sibling relationships
- ▶ How to build a successful step-family
- ▶ Questions to bond over
- ▶ Activities to bond over
- ▶ Building trusting parent-child relationships

Tackling conflict 'out of the heat of the moment' when everyone has calmed down can make a significant difference to family relationships. For persistent problems, how about calling a family meeting to discuss how you can all make things work better?

ENCOURAGING GOOD SIBLING RELATIONSHIPS

'He hit me!', 'No, she hit me!', 'I want to go first', 'No, I want to go first'... multiply that by ten and you've got the kind of squabbles that go on in many a family with two-plus children jostling for position. Yes, it's probably character-building for them to learn to get on but as a parent, playing referee all day can be decidedly wearing.

What you can do

Identify flashpoints

Is there a particular pattern to when your children argue? Perhaps, when they're tired or vying for parental attention? Over a particular game, gadget or 'resource'? Or... if you're especially unlucky, just about everything. You could even keep a diary of arguments for a week or two to see if that helps you spot any patterns.

Set clear rules for areas of contention

Whether it's about whose turn it is on the games console, trampoline or to have the choice of this week's takeaway, having crystal-clear rules will reduce conflict. Write them out and pin them up on the fridge if needed. Have sanctions for not following the rules – such as if they continue to argue, it'll be nobody's turn next time.

Don't step in to mediate too quickly

Let your children try to resolve minor battles themselves (obviously intervene if there's about to be a sibling murder) – it's good for them. Ask 'how could you resolve this?' Encourage them to question what they could do to make things fairer or to work out who should take which turn.

If conflict persists, sit them down when they're calmer

Wait until they've calmed down, then discuss what they think happened, get them to each provide their view without the other being allowed to interrupt, encourage empathy ('How would you have felt if that had been you?') and work out what they might do differently next time.

Try to be fair where possible

Tensions can arise between brothers and sisters if they feel parents – or grandparents – are giving greater amounts of attention, resources or presents to siblings than they are getting. Try to keep things fair.

Watch out for labelling and making comparisons

It's somewhat natural and normal to compare our children but it's important not to make them aware of this. Labelling them 'the clever/sporty/less sporty/shier' sibling can be quite limiting and damage their confidence.

Build some shared interests or activities to bond over

If your kids are quite different, or drifting apart, look to build some common ground – it could be a sport or hobby they both like, a regular visit to the cinema (provided you can find films they both want to see!) or an occasional theme park outing.

Be realistic

A bit of name calling and squabbling is part of growing up with siblings. They can't be best friends all the time, or even friends. Don't despair: kids who fought the most growing up, sometimes end up the closest as adults.

HOW TO BUILD A SUCCESSFUL STEP-FAMILY

More families than ever in the UK now include 'step relationships', be it step-parents or step-siblings too. There are plenty of harmonious and happy step-families out there (despite what the fairy tale stereotypes would have you believe) but of course, equally such relationships can be stressful and need effort and time to build.

What you can do

Have reasonable expectations

We'd all love to think that you, your new partner and any step-kids will live happily ever after right from that first introduction but back in the real world, things are often trickier.

Take your time

Expect a rocky road at least initially as you all get used to each other. This won't happen overnight; it can take years to build a step-family with trust, comfort and stability.

Look for ways to bond (but don't try too hard!)

Identify activities, outings or topics that you can use to break the ice and bond over in your new family unit. It could be anything from a shopping trip to watching a comedy on TV. But don't go too far; teens especially will sniff out any 'trying too hard' desperation and could either find it off-putting or take advantage.

Recognise that you can't replace biological parents

Don't seek to be their new mum or dad or expect your children to view your new partner in that way. Wise step-parents aim to be an extra, caring adult in their step-children's lives, not a parent substitute.

Set house rules that apply to all children

Managing the behaviour and dynamics of two families coming together can be especially tough. Aim to devise one set of house rules that will be enforced by both adults and followed by all children regardless of what goes on with their other parents or has gone before.

Let the main parent take the lead on managing poor behaviour where possible

Particularly in the beginning, it works better to have the main parent discipline their own children – obviously if they are not around, you will still have to step in sometimes. In this scenario it's wise to be slightly more cautious – perhaps the way an aunt or uncle would.

Never talk badly of their other parent

There is nothing to be gained by bad mouthing their mum or dad; it will just create resentment. Keep your opinions out of earshot.

Carry on carving out time for your non-step children

They might be feeling left out or worrying that new family members mean they're less important to you. It's also unfair to expect your own children to suddenly do everything with their new step-parent or step-siblings. Schedule in some activities just for you and your own kids now and then, especially at the start – this will also allow you to talk openly together about how they are feeling.

Don't neglect your relationship

Blending families is hard work – don't lose sight of what brought you and your partner together in the first place and make sure you get time alone together too.

QUESTIONS TO BOND OVER

Run out of conversation topics? Want to share insights and views among family members? Get asking…

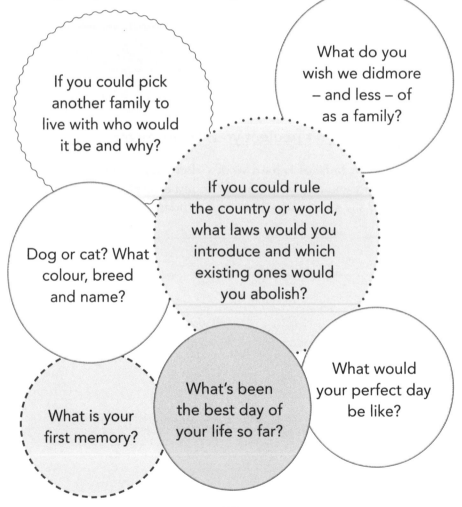

If you could pick another family to live with who would it be and why?

What do you wish we didmore – and less – of as a family?

Dog or cat? What colour, breed and name?

If you could rule the country or world, what laws would you introduce and which existing ones would you abolish?

What is your first memory?

What's been the best day of your life so far?

What would your perfect day be like?

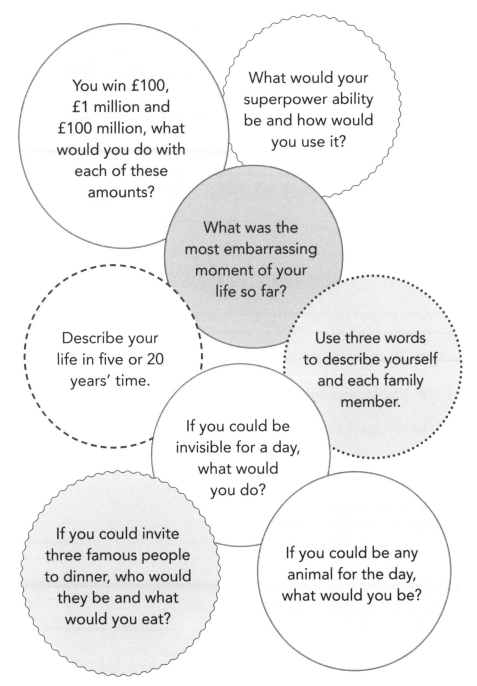

You win £100, £1 million and £100 million, what would you do with each of these amounts?

What would your superpower ability be and how would you use it?

What was the most embarrassing moment of your life so far?

Describe your life in five or 20 years' time.

Use three words to describe yourself and each family member.

If you could be invisible for a day, what would you do?

If you could invite three famous people to dinner, who would they be and what would you eat?

If you could be any animal for the day, what would you be?

ACTIVITIES TO BOND OVER

▶ Roll down a large, grassy hill!

▶ Stargaze somewhere with a great view of the night sky.

▶ Go camping and toast marshmallows on a camp fire (or a barbecue).

▶ Hike up to a place with a beautiful view.

▶ Go to a concert.

▶ Go to a festival.

▶ Learn a language together.

▶ Go wild swimming – in the sea or a river.

▶ Have a water/pillow fight.

▶ Go on a night hike.

BUILDING TRUSTING PARENT– CHILD RELATIONSHIPS

It can be easy to overlook that your relationship with your child should be based on mutual trust and respect. You can use these points as a 'checklist' or just revisit them every so often to keep you on track.

► Never laugh, tease or mock your child about something that genuinely concerns or upsets them.

► If you promise not to tell anyone something your child confides in you, stand by that. In fact, if you promise anything, stick with it wherever possible, unless there's a very good explanation as to why you can't deliver.

► Really listen to what your child is saying. You don't have to agree with them or approve but at least hear them out. If they don't feel listened to, they might not bother telling you next time.

► Appreciate their openness – if your child confides in you, even if you don't like what you're hearing, let them know that you're pleased they felt comfortable talking to you about it.

Family life can be hard sometimes but before you know it, your offspring will be all grown up and largely off doing their own thing. So find time to stop, take a step back and enjoy what you have together now – don't wish away the days. Look up from the screens, stop worrying about what you'll make for dinner and be really present and together.

CHAPTER 9

DIFFICULT TIMES

- ▶ How to help your child through a bereavement
- ▶ Should your children attend a funeral?
- ▶ How to help your child through divorce or separation
- ▶ World events – explaining and providing reassurance

" Being there for each other when times are tough is surely what being a family is all about. "

HOW TO HELP YOUR CHILD THROUGH A BEREAVEMENT

Comforting your child when there's been a bereavement is probably one of the greatest challenges you'll face as a parent, and all at a time when you're probably finding things tough yourself.

What you can do

Seek support

Ask for help for yourself or for your child if they're finding it difficult to talk or you're concerned about the way they are dealing with things. Speak to your GP or contact one of the specialist bereavement charities (try www. winstonswish.org.uk or www.childbereavementuk.org) which offer advice and counselling services.

Encourage talking and show them it's OK to cry or to be upset or sad

Let them know they can talk about things whenever they want and it's fine to show how they feel. Don't think you can't let them see you upset – you don't have to be 'stiff upper lip' strong all the time in front of the children. It's healthy for them to see you're sad too and what they're feeling is normal in the circumstances.

Deal with questions openly

Bereavement (and learning someone is terminally ill) can trigger questions about death from children. It's important to show that death is part of life. If you simply don't know the answer to something they ask, don't be afraid to make comments such as, 'it's hard for me to understand too' or that you actually don't know.

Keep a close eye on their reaction

Bereaved children behave in different ways. Even the same child can react very differently at varying times. They might be fine and asking for dinner at 6 p.m. and then dissolving into tears by bedtime. Some might start wetting the bed, not eating, or waking at night when they haven't done so for years. This is all normal, if difficult for you. If problems persist, again, seek support via your GP – counselling might be beneficial.

Make it clear it was not their fault

Younger children might believe they were somehow to blame for what happened. Their active imaginations mean that there can be quite obscure ways they think this has worked, for instance if only they had done better at school or not shouted at you etc. the person wouldn't have died. Reassure them that nothing they said or did was the cause.

Avoid euphemisms for death – they can confuse younger children

Saying something like 'Grandma has gone to sleep now' could make a younger child afraid of going to sleep. Explaining that the person has 'gone away' might make them think they left voluntarily, leading to fears others will die if they're away from them.

Help them to remember

Creating a memory box can work well for primary school age children. They will be able to look at it when sad or when they want to remember their loved one. It could include poems or pictures they create, mementoes of their time together and photos.

Prepare them for a death that's expected

It's tempting sometimes not to tell children about a relative or friend who is terminally ill (where it isn't otherwise obvious) but it can be helpful in the long term to be prepared and have a chance to say goodbye, even if it seems harder in the short term.

Keep to their normal routine where possible

The certainty of knowing dinner will still be at seven and bedtime at the usual hour is comforting for most grieving children.

SHOULD YOUR CHILD ATTEND A FUNERAL?

There's no right answer to this – it depends largely on the nature of your child, their age and relationship to the person who died. On the one hand funerals can leave some children even more upset but for others they help them understand the person is gone. They might also find it beneficial to be with family and friends who are mourning.

Take your child's lead

Do they want to go? If they've never been to a funeral, explain what will happen so they can decide.

For close family, let them get involved

If it's someone close and it feels appropriate, you might want to include your child in some aspects of planning the funeral (e.g. choosing music) or they might want to participate in the service – perhaps writing something that can be read out (by themselves or someone else).

Have a relative or friend on hand at the service if you'll struggle

If you will be very upset, it's worth having a trusted family member or friend sit with your child. They can explain what's going on if needed, reassure them or take them out if they feel they'd rather not carry on part way through.

Look at alternatives if your child doesn't attend

If you or your child decides they aren't going to go to the funeral, bereavement experts suggest having some sort of memorial or ceremony for children to participate in, whether it's planting a tree or sending balloons into the sky with a poem or message attached on tags.

HOW TO HELP YOUR CHILD THROUGH DIVORCE OR SEPARATION

Parenting through divorce or separation can be complicated and draining. Even if they've listened to years of arguments, and felt the tension between you and your soon-to-be ex, it can still be shocking and upsetting when they hear their parents are separating.

What you can do

Break the news together if possible

Not easy if things are fraught between you but ideally tell your child together. If you can't for whatever reason, ensure that both parents have chance to discuss the situation with them.

There's no right thing to say here

This is not an easy conversation – there's no magic wording someone else can provide, however it's wise to be honest in an age-appropriate way. That does not mean 'I hate your mother/father and can't stand them' but a more measured version, without too many details. So perhaps, 'we're arguing too much and although we've tried to sort this out, we can't and think it would be better for everyone to not live together anymore.'

Choose your timing

If you can, tell them sooner rather than later so they have time to adjust to changes within the household such as one of you moving out, but only once initial plans are firmed up.

Make it clear that they are not to blame

Younger children especially can be prone to thinking they've done something to cause the separation. Let them know one hundred per cent that this is not the case.

Offer masses of reassurance

Whether they're little ones or teens, children whose parents are separating will need to hear that both of you will continue to love them and are going to see them (assuming the latter is the case).

Talk about practicalities

Your child might worry about how much they will see each parent, living arrangements, changes to school, moving house, not seeing grandparents, friends or even pets. Be honest if you can't answer all their questions yet, but do try to resolve things as promptly as you can.

Keep as much stability as possible

If you can keep as many other aspects of their lives the same as 'before', it will help them through the transition.

Look out for reactions – they might not be obvious initially

Children's responses to parental separation vary depending on their personality, relationships with each parent, and the nature of the separation. Reactions can include denial, frustration, anger, blame or silence. There may be an initial response and then quite a different one later on when they've digested things.

Keep talking

Take your child's lead as they won't always want to discuss it all but keep checking in on how they're feeling and chatting together when they are keen to open up.

Don't bad-mouth your ex to your child

Children shouldn't feel they have to take sides. Let off steam with friends or relatives out of earshot of your child, or seek professional support if you are finding it difficult to hide your anger and frustration.

GOLDEN RULES FOR POST-DIVORCE PARENTING

▶ Don't use your child to spy on what your ex is up to.

▶ Avoid criticising your ex-partner in front of your children – hard if you're feeling bitter, angry or abandoned but important for the sake of their relationship with them.

▶ Don't use your child as a weapon to punish your ex, for instance by limiting access or contact.

▶ Don't try to buy affection, get one up on your ex or try to assuage any guilt you feel by spoiling your child with material items or *too* much attention – it won't be good for them even if it's tempting or feels like the right thing to do.

▶ Do your best to agree on your approach to parenting – challenging of course if you're at loggerheads, but consistency will really help your child if you can be 'on the same page'.

It's not parental separation per se that is harmful to children but the level of conflict between their parents that they experience. Clearly if you're separating, keeping things civil can be challenging, but ideally try to shelter your child from arguments, bad-mouthing and resentments as much as you can.

CONCLUSION

People often say they want the best for their children but perhaps we should say we want the best for them for their whole lives. If there's one thing to keep in mind then, it's that our role as parents is not raising children but really to raise happy, well-functioning adults.

ACKNOWLEDGEMENTS

Thanks once more to the team at Summersdale, particularly Claire, Anna and Dean, and to assorted colleagues, friends and family who score 10/10 as my sounding boards – you know who you are. Finally, to my mum for being a super proofreader (your rigorous grammatical education in the 1950s and 1960s has its uses to this day) and to Luca for being my chance to check all this stuff actually works.

NEW Old-Fashioned Fashioned PARENTING

A GUIDE TO HELP YOU FIND THE BALANCE BETWEEN TRADITIONAL AND MODERN PARENTING

LIAT HUGHES JOSHI

NEW OLD-FASHIONED PARENTING

A Guide to Help You Find the Balance between Traditional and Modern Parenting

Liat Hughes Joshi

£10.99
Paperback
ISBN: 978-1-84953-672-1

There's been a revolution in the family; it's now all about the kids.

We've moved on from children being 'seen and not heard', but we're now plagued with the worry of ending up with 'that child' – the one who's running amok and is ill-prepared for life.

This book combines contemporary and traditional child-rearing methods, bringing fresh thinking to some of the essential parenting issues of our time:

- Managing screen use
- Encouraging independence
- Finding the balance between school and play
- Compromising between parenting that's pushy and not involved enough
- Establishing the 'best of both worlds' approach that works in the modern world for modern families.

In this manifesto of new old-fashioned parenting there's no pandering, no spoiling, and definitely no dinosaur-shaped chicken nuggets at dinner time.

HOW TO
UNPLUG
YOUR CHILD

101 WAYS TO HELP YOUR KIDS TURN OFF
THEIR GADGETS AND ENJOY REAL LIFE

LIAT HUGHES JOSHI

HOW TO UNPLUG YOUR CHILD

101 Ways to Help Your Kids Turn Off Their Gadgets and Enjoy Real Life

Liat Hughes Joshi

£5.99
Paperback
ISBN: 978-1-84953-719-3

This sanity-saving collection of ideas and inspiration will help your children swap the screen for the sunshine and start getting more out of life. Split into bite-sized chapters, from fun indoors to activities on the go, food and cooking to science and nature, this book is packed with activities for all ages of children from preschoolers to even the most jaded, screen-obsessed teens and the kid in all of us too. *How to Unplug Your Child* will give you and your kids a host of things to do after school, at the weekend and during those long holidays.

If you're interested in finding out
more about our books, find us on Facebook
at **Summersdale Publishers** and follow
us on Twitter at **@Summersdale**.

www.summersdale.com

Image credits